Ellis Alder

Marie Antoinette, A Biography: A Life of Luxury, Scandal, and Tragedy

Table of Contents

Chapter 1: The Austrian Archduchess: Early Years

Chapter 2: A Marriage of Alliances: The Franco-Austrian Union

Chapter 3: Life at Versailles: Adjusting to French Court

Chapter 4: Queen of France: The Rise of Marie Antoinette

Chapter 5: Indulgence and Extravagance: The Height of Luxury

Chapter 6: The Seeds of Discontent: Political Turmoil

Chapter 7: Family and Personal Struggles

Chapter 8: The Revolution Begins: Fall from Grace

Chapter 9: The Imprisoned Queen: Trials and Tribulations

Chapter 10: The Final Days: Execution and Legacy

Chapter 11: Myth vs. Reality: The Legend of Marie Antoinette

Chapter 12: Reflections on a Life of Contrasts

Chapter 1: The Austrian Archduchess: Early Years

Marie Antoinette was born on November 2, 1755, at the Schönbrunn Palace in Vienna, a magnificent baroque structure that served as the summer residence of the Habsburgs. The air was brisk with the approach of winter, and the grandeur of the palace mirrored the expectations surrounding the birth of a royal child. She was the fifteenth child of Empress Maria Theresa and Emperor Francis I, a union that had produced a remarkable lineage indicative of Habsburg power, yet Marie Antoinette would find herself standing apart from her siblings, marked by both privilege and the weight of expectation.

As the archduchess of Austria, Marie Antoinette was born into a world of opulence and authority, yet her arrival was steeped in the realities of political strategy. Her mother, Maria Theresa, was a formidable ruler who had strengthened the Habsburg dynasty through a series of shrewd alliances and marriages. The birth of yet another daughter could have easily been viewed as a disappointment, yet it was precisely this multitude of offspring that allowed her to craft alliances across Europe. Marie Antoinette was destined to be a pawn in a game of dynastic politics, her worth measured not in her individuality but in her ability to unite kingdoms.

The court of Vienna, known for its elaborate ceremonies and strict protocols, was a world unto itself. From an early age, Marie Antoinette was enveloped in the rituals of the Habsburg court, where every moment was choreographed to perfection. The empress, a mother deeply committed to both her family and her empire, ensured that her children were raised with the knowledge that they were not simply heirs to a throne but also future representatives of their house. As Marie Antoinette took her first breaths, she was already being prepared for the complexities of her future role.

Maria Theresa was a progressive ruler who believed in the education of her daughters as well as her sons, a principle that was somewhat revolutionary for the time. The young archduchess was surrounded by tutors and scholars who would instill in her the knowledge necessary for a queen. She learned languages, history, and the arts, her education designed not only to equip her for life at court but also to enable her to navigate the treacherous waters of European politics. Despite her privileged upbringing, the weight of expectation hung heavy over her. She was trained to embody the virtues of a perfect queen—grace, poise, and an unwavering sense of duty.

The early years of Marie Antoinette's life were punctuated by the joys and challenges of childhood, set against the backdrop of the Habsburg court's opulence. She was often seen playing in the lush gardens of Schönbrunn, where the vibrant colors of the flowers seemed to echo the liveliness of her spirit. Yet, even in those idyllic moments, the realities of her future loomed large. Each game, each laugh, was tinged with the knowledge that her life would one day be dictated by the expectations of her family and the demands of her status.

As the youngest daughter, Marie Antoinette often found herself in the shadow of her older siblings. Her sisters were married off to secure alliances, while her brothers were groomed to inherit the family legacy. In this environment, she was both cherished and overlooked, a paradox that would shape her character. She craved affection and validation, often seeking the company of her mother and siblings, hoping to carve out her own space within the expansive and sometimes suffocating world of the Habsburgs.

However, the birth of Marie Antoinette also coincided with a period of significant upheaval in Europe. The Seven Years' War had recently concluded, and its aftermath left many European powers in a state of flux. Austria, under Maria Theresa's leadership, was striving to recover from the losses sustained during the conflict. It was a time when alliances were critical, and marriages were not merely romantic unions but calculated strategies to secure peace and stability. Thus, Marie Antoinette's life was predetermined by the political landscape that surrounded her, a fact that would follow her throughout her life.

The court's incessant pressure and the ever-watchful gaze of her mother instilled in her a sense of duty, but it also ignited a yearning for freedom and self-expression. The young archduchess found solace in music and dance, her passion for the arts becoming a significant aspect of her identity. She would often escape the formalities of court life through the melodies of the harpsichord or the rhythm of the waltz, moments when she could momentarily shed the weight of her title and simply be a girl lost in the beauty of life.

As she approached adolescence, the reality of her future became increasingly clear. It was not merely her duty to marry and produce heirs; she was to be a symbol of Franco-Austrian relations, a bridge between two powerful nations. The decision to marry her off to Louis-Auguste, the future King of France, was rooted in the necessity of forging a stronger alliance between the two countries. The prospect of her marriage loomed on the horizon, a distant echo of the grand ambitions her mother held for her.

In the years leading up to her marriage, Marie Antoinette's life was a delicate balancing act of familial loyalty and personal desire. She learned the intricacies of diplomacy, but her heart yearned for the simplicity of genuine connection. The opulence of her surroundings often felt like a gilded cage, and it was this dichotomy—a life of luxury intertwined with the harsh realities of politics—that would come to define her existence.

Thus, Marie Antoinette's early years were marked by both privilege and pressure. Born into a royal family that demanded perfection, she was nurtured in the lavish halls of Schönbrunn, where beauty and duty were inextricably linked. While the world outside her palace was rife with conflict and intrigue, her formative years in Vienna would lay the groundwork for a life that would oscillate between the heights of glory and the depths of tragedy. The archduchess, destined for greatness, was about to embark on a journey that would transform her from a naive child into one of history's most scrutinized queens.

Marie Antoinette's childhood in the Habsburg Court was a tapestry woven with threads of privilege, expectation, and the rigid constraints of royal upbringing. Born on November 2, 1755, in Vienna, she was the fifteenth child of Empress Maria Theresa and Emperor Francis I. From the moment of her birth, it was clear that her life would be one of immense scrutiny and high stakes. The Habsburg dynasty, with its sprawling network of alliances and rivalries, viewed each child not merely as a member of the family but as a pawn in the game of European politics.

In the opulent halls of the Schönbrunn Palace, Marie Antoinette spent her early years surrounded by luxury. The palace itself was a marvel of Baroque architecture, with grand ballrooms, lush gardens, and meticulously appointed rooms that spoke to the wealth and power of the Habsburgs. Yet, within these gilded walls, the life of a royal child was anything but carefree. The court was a realm where decorum reigned supreme, and the education of a future queen was a matter of utmost importance.

From a young age, Marie Antoinette was surrounded by tutors and governesses, each tasked with instilling in her the virtues expected of a royal. The emphasis was placed not only on academic learning but also on the cultural arts. She was taught languages—German, French, and Italian—alongside music, dance, and etiquette. The Habsburgs prided themselves on their cultural sophistication, and Marie Antoinette was expected to embody this standard. Her mother, Empress Maria Theresa, was especially vigilant in ensuring that her daughters were well-prepared for their future roles as queens and consorts. The lessons were rigorous and often demanding, designed to mold them into the ideal royal figures.

Amidst the strictness of her education, Marie Antoinette's childhood was not devoid of warmth or affection. Her mother was known for her formidable presence, yet she also had a tender side that shaped her children's upbringing. Maria Theresa, while a stern ruler, was also a loving mother who devoted considerable time to her offspring. She emphasized the importance of family and the need for her daughters to support each other in their future roles. The bond between Marie Antoinette and her siblings was nurtured, creating a close-knit alliance that would prove invaluable as they navigated their respective destinies.

However, while family ties were strong, the atmosphere of the Habsburg Court was also fraught with tension. The specter of political alliances loomed over every interaction. Each daughter was a bargaining chip in her mother's grand strategy to strengthen the Habsburg influence across Europe. Marie Antoinette was no exception; her marriage was already being arranged before she fully understood its implications. The notion of being married off to solidify alliances weighed heavily on the young princess, though the magnitude of her future responsibilities remained a distant concept in her youthful mind.

Despite the pressures of court life, Marie Antoinette found moments of joy and escape. She would often retreat to the gardens of Schönbrunn, where she could indulge in the simple pleasures of nature. The sprawling grounds offered her a sanctuary away from the rigid expectations of court. Here, she could roam freely, picking flowers and daydreaming about a life unfettered by the chains of duty. The gardens were not merely a backdrop for her childhood; they were a canvas for her imagination, a space where she could envision her own identity outside the confines of royal expectation.

As she grew older, Marie Antoinette began to experience the complexities of court life more acutely. The incessant scrutiny of courtiers and the constant competition for favor made her acutely aware of her status as a royal. She witnessed the intricate dance of power and influence played out before her, as various factions vied for the attention of their mother and the Emperor. The court was a place of both camaraderie and rivalry, where friendships were often laced with ambition. It was a lesson that would serve her well in her future as Queen of France.

At the heart of her education was the cultivation of grace and poise. Marie Antoinette was taught to navigate the labyrinthine customs of courtly life, learning to smile through the most challenging of circumstances. The court demanded congeniality, and she understood that her demeanor could sway public opinion—a skill that would become both a blessing and a curse in her later years. The dichotomy of her existence was stark; while she was groomed to be a symbol of regal elegance, her personal desires often clashed with the expectations placed upon her.

As she approached the age of adolescence, the pressures of her impending marriage loomed larger. The Habsburg Court's political machinations were relentless, and the prospect of securing a favorable union was both exciting and daunting. With the burden of expectation pressing down on her, Marie Antoinette's childhood gradually transformed into a preparation for her role as a queen consort. Her upbringing, once filled with the innocent joys of youth, began to morph into a series of calculated steps toward fulfilling a destiny not entirely of her choosing.

Ultimately, the childhood of Marie Antoinette in the Habsburg Court was marked by a delicate balance between privilege and obligation. While she enjoyed the luxuries of her royal status, she was ever aware of the chains that accompanied her birthright. The lessons learned during these formative years would shape her character, preparing her for the turbulent waters of her future in France. As she would soon discover, the journey from the gilded halls of Vienna to the opulent courts of Versailles would not only challenge her resolve but also redefine the very essence of her identity as a queen.

Marie Antoinette's education was meticulously crafted, a reflection of her status as an archduchess in the Habsburg dynasty. Her formative years were steeped in the traditions of the Austrian court, where the lessons imparted were as much about the art of governance as they were about the nuances of social etiquette. Born into a family that valued both intellectual and cultural refinement, Marie Antoinette was shaped by a curriculum designed not only to prepare her for her eventual role as queen but also to equip her with the tools necessary to navigate the complexities of European politics.

From a young age, Marie Antoinette was surrounded by the grandeur of the Habsburg court, where she was expected to exhibit grace and poise. Her education was overseen by a cadre of tutors and governesses, each selected for their expertise and ability to instill the values and knowledge deemed essential for a future queen. Among them was Madame de Brionne, who took charge of her early education, ensuring that the young archduchess was well-versed in the arts of conversation and comportment. The emphasis on manners was paramount; she was taught to walk with elegance, to speak with clarity, and to engage with others in a manner that reflected her noble status.

Language was also a significant component of her education. Fluent in both German and French from an early age, Marie Antoinette learned to appreciate the subtleties of these languages, as they would serve her not only in her personal life but also in her diplomatic endeavors. The ability to converse with foreign dignitaries and to understand the nuances of political discourse was vital, particularly as she was destined to become the queen of France. Additionally, her education included lessons in Italian and Spanish, expanding her linguistic repertoire and enhancing her status as a potential mediator between nations.

While language and etiquette formed the foundation of her education, Marie Antoinette was also exposed to the world of art and culture. Under the tutelage of skilled artists and musicians, she developed a profound appreciation for the arts. Music, in particular, played a significant role in her upbringing; she was taught to play the harpsichord and was encouraged to sing. These pursuits were not merely hobbies but were seen as essential qualifications for a queen, who was expected to patronize the arts and inspire cultural growth within her realm. Furthermore, her exposure to literature and philosophy fostered a love for reading, allowing her to engage with the great thinkers of her time, even if her understanding of their ideas was primarily superficial.

The education of Marie Antoinette was not without its challenges. The pressures of court life meant that she was constantly under scrutiny, and her tutors were tasked with molding her into an ideal representation of Habsburg virtue. This relentless pursuit of perfection often left little room for personal expression or individuality. The young archduchess was aware that her every action would be judged, not just by her family but by the entire court and, eventually, by the French people. This pressure instilled a sense of duty within her, a recognition that her role was not simply to fulfill her own desires but to serve the interests of her family and her country.

As a member of the Habsburg dynasty, Marie Antoinette was also taught the intricacies of political alliances and the importance of marriage as a tool for diplomacy. Her mother, Empress Maria Theresa, was particularly invested in her daughters' futures, emphasizing the notion that their marriages would create bonds that could stabilize the precarious political landscape of Europe. In this context, Marie Antoinette's education extended beyond the confines of the classroom; it was a real-time lesson in the art of statecraft, as she observed the relationships between monarchs and the delicate balance of power that defined European politics.

Despite the rigorous structure of her education, moments of warmth and affection existed within her upbringing. Her relationship with her siblings, particularly with her beloved sister, Maria Carolina, provided a respite from the demands of court life. These bonds offered Marie Antoinette a glimpse of the joys of companionship and loyalty, aspects of life that would later prove crucial during her time in France. The support of her family instilled in her a sense of identity and belonging, even as the weight of her royal duties loomed large.

As Marie Antoinette approached her teenage years, her education began to shift in focus. The lessons became more directly applicable to her future role as queen. She learned about the governance of a kingdom, the responsibilities that would fall upon her shoulders, and the expectations of a queen consort. Discussions of state affairs and the intricacies of court politics replaced the more whimsical subjects of childhood. It was a sobering realization that the idyllic world of her youth was giving way to the harsh realities of responsibility and sacrifice.

With her marriage to Louis-Auguste, the future Louis XVI of France, on the horizon, the final phase of her education was characterized by an urgency to prepare her for the challenges ahead. The lessons from her tutors became more practical, focusing on the realities of French court life and the expectations that would accompany her new status. Marie Antoinette studied the history of France, familiarizing herself with the customs and traditions of her future home, all while grappling with the knowledge that her life was about to change irrevocably.

The education of Marie Antoinette, therefore, was not merely an academic endeavor; it was a carefully orchestrated preparation for a life that would be filled with luxury, but also with scandal and tragedy. She emerged from her upbringing as a product of her environment—noble, well-educated, and poised to take on the mantle of queen. Yet, the lessons learned in the court of Vienna would prove to be both a boon and a burden as she stepped into the tumultuous world of the French monarchy, where the very qualities that defined her might be scrutinized and challenged in ways she could scarcely imagine. As her journey unfolded, the contrast between the sheltered archduchess of Vienna and the queen of France would become starkly evident, setting the stage for a life that would be marked by both opulence and upheaval.

Chapter 2: A Marriage of Alliances: The Franco-Austrian Union

In the heart of the 18th century, the political landscape of Europe was fraught with tension, alliances, and the ever-present specter of war. The Habsburgs of Austria and the Bourbons of France, two of the most powerful dynasties on the continent, had long been rivals, their animosities flaring up in numerous conflicts. However, as the threat of British naval dominance loomed and the fear of Prussian expansion grew, a radical shift in strategy emerged—a realization that the future of both kingdoms could rest upon a single, strategic marriage. Thus, the union of Marie Antoinette and Louis-Auguste, the heir to the French throne, was conceived, a diplomatic maneuver designed to forge an alliance that would secure peace and mutual benefit.

Empress Maria Theresa, Marie Antoinette's mother, was the architect of this alliance. A formidable and astute ruler, she understood that a marriage between her daughter and the future King of France could serve as a powerful deterrent against Austria's enemies. In the austere halls of the Schönbrunn Palace, she orchestrated the negotiations with a meticulousness that revealed her political acumen. Letters flew between Vienna and Paris, with both courtly and familial interests at stake. The match was not merely about love; it was about stabilizing an ever-shifting balance of power in Europe.

The negotiations were layered with complexity. France, still reeling from the aftermath of the War of the Austrian Succession, was eager to solidify its position in Europe. The marriage was seen as a means to cement peace and foster goodwill between the two nations. However, the path to this union was fraught with obstacles, including the skepticism of the French court and the deep-seated rivalries that existed within its ranks. Some members of the French nobility questioned the wisdom of aligning with Austria, a nation that had long been viewed with suspicion. To assuage these fears, Maria Theresa deftly painted a portrait of her daughter that highlighted her virtues: her beauty, charm, and grace, all qualities that could win over the hearts of the French people.

As the negotiations progressed, Marie Antoinette remained largely shielded from the political machinations surrounding her. Instead, she was instructed in the arts of diplomacy and propriety, preparing her for the role she would soon assume. The young archduchess often spent her days in the company of her siblings, engaged in leisure activities, oblivious to the weight of her future. Yet, there was an awareness that her life was about to change dramatically.

The formalities of the marriage negotiations were further complicated by the deep-rooted traditions of both courts. The Habsburgs were renowned for their elaborate ceremonies, while the Bourbons had their own expectations of grandeur. The engagement had to be celebrated with a magnificence befitting both families, and this required careful planning. Maria Theresa took personal charge of this endeavor, ensuring that every detail was executed flawlessly. The royal families exchanged gifts, from ornate jewelry to lavish tapestries, each item symbolizing the merging of two great houses.

As the date of the wedding approached, Marie Antoinette received an influx of advice from her mother, who counseled her on the importance of adaptability and charm. Maria Theresa understood that the success of the marriage depended not only on the union of two individuals but on the ability of her daughter to navigate the intricate and often treacherous waters of the French court. The archduchess was to become a beacon of hope for peace between two nations, and Maria Theresa's letters were filled with reminders of her duty and the weight of her responsibilities.

The grand journey from Vienna to France was a spectacle in itself, designed to showcase the significance of the marriage. Marie Antoinette traveled in a lavishly adorned carriage, surrounded by a retinue of attendants, each tasked with ensuring her comfort and safety. The journey took several weeks, with stops that allowed her to bask in the adoration of the crowds that gathered along the route. The people of the towns she passed through were eager to glimpse the future queen, and her beauty captivated all who beheld her. Yet, amidst the excitement, there lingered a sense of trepidation; she was leaving her family and homeland behind, stepping into a world that was both exhilarating and intimidating.

Upon her arrival in France, Marie Antoinette was met with a mixture of enthusiasm and skepticism. The French court, with its elaborate rules and intricate hierarchies, was daunting. She was not merely marrying a prince; she was entering a realm where her actions would be scrutinized and her every move analyzed. The realities of court life would soon begin to shape her identity, but for now, she was the bride adorned in finery, poised to fulfill her role as a symbol of unity between two powerful nations.

The wedding itself was a grand affair, characterized by opulence and pageantry that reflected the significance of the union. The ceremony was steeped in tradition, with rituals designed to bless the marriage and ensure its longevity. As Marie Antoinette stood alongside her husband, the future Louis XVI, the weight of history loomed over them. This marriage, conceived in the crucible of political necessity, was not just a joining of two hearts; it was a cornerstone upon which the future of France and Austria would be built.

Yet, as Marie Antoinette embarked on this new chapter, she could not foresee the tumultuous journey that lay ahead. The hopes of nations rested upon her shoulders, and the delicate balance of power in Europe would soon be tested in ways that would challenge not only her marriage but her very existence. The negotiations that had culminated in this grand union were just the beginning of a life filled with luxury, scandal, and, ultimately, tragedy.

As the sun rose over the sprawling landscape of the Habsburg Empire, a palpable sense of anticipation filled the air. The day marveled at the opulence of Vienna, where the grand palaces stood as testaments to the power and prestige of the Habsburgs. Yet, in the heart of this splendid city, a young archduchess was preparing to embark on a journey that would alter the course of her life and that of an entire nation. Marie Antoinette, the youngest daughter of Empress Maria Theresa and Emperor Francis I, was to leave her homeland, her family, and the familiar comforts of the Austrian court to marry Louis-Auguste, the Dauphin of France. This union, forged through political necessity, was designed to cement the Franco-Austrian alliance and bring stability to a Europe teetering on the brink of conflict.

The grand journey to France began on April 21, 1770. The streets of Vienna bustled with life as Marie Antoinette, dressed in a sumptuous gown adorned with intricate lace and fine silk, stepped into the carriage that would take her away from all she had ever known. Her heart raced with a blend of excitement and trepidation, for she was not merely a bride; she was a symbol of hope, a living embodiment of the fragile peace her marriage aimed to secure. Surrounded by her family and an entourage of courtiers, she was bid farewell by her mother, who, though proud, could not hide the sorrow in her eyes.

As the carriage rolled through the city gates, Marie Antoinette caught her last glimpse of Vienna, her home since birth. The familiar sights blurred into a tapestry of memories—the gardens of Schönbrunn, the grandeur of the Hofburg Palace, and the laughter of her siblings. The journey ahead would take her through lands both foreign and familiar, yet she felt the weight of her royal duty pressing upon her shoulders.

The route to France was meticulously planned, with stops at various courts and palaces along the way. Each stop was an opportunity for Marie Antoinette to be received with pomp and splendor, a reminder of her status and the importance of her mission. The first leg of her journey took her to the picturesque town of Innsbruck, where she was greeted by the local nobility. Here, the festivities were grand, with feasts that showcased the culinary delights of the region, and balls where the music echoed late into the night. Despite the revelry, Marie Antoinette felt the bittersweet pangs of leaving her homeland—a land she would soon become a stranger to.

Continuing her journey, the entourage made its way through the majestic Alps, where the snow-capped peaks loomed in stark contrast to the lush valleys below. The breathtaking beauty of the mountains stirred something deep within her. Yet, as they traversed the treacherous passes, Marie Antoinette was reminded of the precariousness of her situation. The winding roads were fraught with danger, and her heart fluttered at the thought of what awaited her on the other side.

Upon reaching the French border, a wave of excitement rippled through the entourage. The moment they crossed into French territory, they were met with a display of grandeur that was distinctively French. The countryside transformed into a tapestry of rolling vineyards and blooming lavender fields, each village they passed adorned with banners celebrating the arrival of their future queen. The locals gathered in droves to catch a glimpse of the young archduchess, their faces a mixture of curiosity and awe. Marie Antoinette, accustomed to the adoration of the Austrian court, felt a surge of confidence. Yet, in the back of her mind, a whisper of uncertainty lingered—what would her new life entail?

As they approached the city of Metz, the atmosphere became increasingly festive. The streets were lined with flowers, and the air was thick with the scent of freshly baked bread and sweet pastries. Here, Marie Antoinette was welcomed with a grand procession. The townsfolk, adorned in their best garments, cheered her name, their voices rising in a chorus of hope and expectation. The young archduchess smiled and waved, her heart swelling with the excitement of her new role, yet tinged with the realization that she was leaving behind the only life she had ever known.

In Metz, the celebrations continued for several days, allowing Marie Antoinette to rest and reflect on her journey thus far. It was here that she began to understand the profound implications of her marriage. She was not simply marrying a man; she was marrying a kingdom. Every decision she would make, every gesture she would perform, would be scrutinized through the lens of public expectation and political necessity. As she donned the elegant attire gifted to her by the people of Metz, she recognized that she was stepping into a role that would demand both grace and resilience.

The journey then resumed, taking her toward the grand capital of Paris. As they approached the city, the excitement reached fever pitch. The royal entourage was met with an elaborate welcome. The streets of Paris were transformed into a magnificent stage, adorned with flowers and ribbons. As Marie Antoinette entered the city, she was struck by the vibrancy of life that surrounded her. The bustling markets, the laughter of children, and the artistry of the street performers created an atmosphere that was both exhilarating and intimidating.

On May 16, 1770, Marie Antoinette finally arrived at the gates of Versailles, the opulent palace that would be her new home. The grandeur of the estate took her breath away; it was a symbol of the absolute power of the French monarchy. Yet, even amidst the gilded halls and sumptuous gardens, she felt a profound sense of isolation. The expectations placed upon her weighed heavily, and the realities of court life loomed ahead.

As she stepped from her carriage, the cheers of the courtiers and the commoners echoed around her, a cacophony of voices celebrating her arrival. Little did she know that this grand journey, which had promised a life of luxury and power, would soon entangle her in a web of scandal, political strife, and ultimately, tragedy. The path she had begun to tread was fraught with challenges that would test her spirit and redefine her legacy as the Queen of France.

The day of the royal wedding arrived, heralded by a cacophony of bells ringing throughout the grand city of Versailles. The opulence of the occasion was matched only by the grandeur of the palace itself, a fitting backdrop for the union that would forever alter the course of French and Austrian history. Marie Antoinette, dressed in a gown of exquisite silk adorned with intricate lace and sparkling jewels, could hardly contain her excitement and trepidation as she prepared to step into a new life as the Queen of France.

Her wedding to Louis-Auguste, the Dauphin of France, was not merely a romantic affair; it was a carefully orchestrated political alliance designed to fortify the bond between France and Austria. For Marie, this day was laden with expectations and responsibilities. She was acutely aware that her marriage was intended to heal the rifts between two powerful nations, which had long been marked by rivalry and conflict. As she gazed into the ornate mirror, she understood that her role transcended personal desires; she was now a symbol of hope and unity, a living embodiment of her mother's ambitions for peace.

The ceremony took place in the opulent Chapel of Versailles, where the air was thick with the scent of fresh flowers and the excited whispers of courtiers. As she walked down the aisle, she was met with a sea of eyes—nobles, dignitaries, and foreign ambassadors who had gathered to witness the union. The grandeur of the occasion was not lost on her; every detail had been meticulously planned, from the lavish floral arrangements to the gilded decorations that glimmered in the candlelight.

Louis-Auguste awaited her at the altar, his demeanor calm but his heart racing. He was a shy and reserved young man, accustomed to the shadows of the court rather than the spotlight that now surrounded him. Yet, he found solace in Marie's presence; her beauty and vivacity captivated him, and he hoped that together they could navigate the complexities of their royal duties. The vows they exchanged were steeped in tradition, promising fidelity and loyalty, but beneath the surface lay the weight of the expectations that would soon bear down on them.

In the days that followed the wedding, the newlyweds embarked on a series of public celebrations that showcased their union and solidified their status as the future monarchs of France. The streets of Paris were filled with jubilant crowds, who cheered and tossed flowers as the royal carriage traversed the city. The spectacle was a breathtaking display of grandeur, but it was also a reminder of the challenges that lay ahead. The lavish festivities, while meant to foster goodwill among the subjects, were met with mixed reactions; beneath the surface of celebration, there was simmering discontent among the populace.

Marie quickly became aware of the expectations placed upon her as a young queen. She was thrust into the world of court politics, where alliances were fickle, and rivalries simmered just beneath the surface. The intricate web of relationships at Versailles was as complex as the gowns she wore, and she soon found herself navigating the treacherous waters of court life. Her marriage to Louis-Auguste, while initially a source of hope, began to reveal the inherent challenges of their roles.

As she settled into her new life, Marie sought to find her footing within the rigid structure of the French court. She hosted lavish balls and soirées, embracing the role of a social arbiter. Her natural charm and vivacious spirit won her many friends among the courtiers, and she quickly became a beloved figure at Versailles. However, as her popularity grew, so did the whispers of dissent. The extravagant lifestyles of the royal family stood in stark contrast to the struggles faced by ordinary French citizens, and Marie found herself increasingly scrutinized.

In the months that followed the wedding, Marie became aware of the growing tension between her husband and the court. Louis-Auguste, now King Louis XVI, was a man of deep thought and conviction, yet he often struggled to assert his authority. The weight of the crown pressed heavily upon him, and Marie felt an ache of empathy for the man she had married. She endeavored to support him, even as she grappled with her own insecurities and the relentless pressure from the court.

Marie's first years as queen were marked by both triumph and turmoil. The couple welcomed their first child, a daughter named Marie-Thérèse, in 1778, a moment that momentarily dispelled the clouds of uncertainty hovering over their reign. The birth was celebrated with great fanfare, and for a fleeting moment, joy enveloped the royal couple. Yet, motherhood brought with it new responsibilities and expectations, further complicating Marie's life at court.

As she embraced her role as a mother, Marie also sought to carve out a space for herself in the vast landscape of French society. The Petit Trianon, a charming retreat situated within the grounds of Versailles, became her sanctuary. Here, she could escape the grandeur and rigidity of court life, indulging in her passions for art, music, and fashion. The Petit Trianon was a reflection of her personality—a place of intimacy and beauty where she could breathe freely, away from the prying eyes of the court.

However, the whispers of discontent continued to grow, and with each lavish banquet and extravagant gown, the seeds of resentment among the French populace deepened. Marie's life, once filled with the promise of love and happiness, began to fracture under the weight of expectation and public scrutiny. The marriage that had begun as a symbol of hope for peace was now seen by many as emblematic of excess and disconnect from the struggles of the common people.

As Marie Antoinette navigated her new life as Queen of France, she found herself at a crossroads—a collision of personal desires, royal duty, and the burgeoning discontent of the nation. The foundation of her reign was being tested, and the challenges of her marriage would soon unfold in ways she could never have anticipated. As the shadows of history loomed ever closer, Marie realized that the path ahead would be fraught with trials, forcing her to confront the complexities of her identity as both a queen and a woman in a world dominated by power and politics.

Chapter 3: Life at Versailles: Adjusting to French Court

As Marie Antoinette arrived in France, she was thrust into the dazzling yet treacherous world of the Versailles court, a realm that was as intricate as it was beautiful. The palace, a magnificent symbol of absolute monarchy, was a stage where not only the politics of the nation played out but also the delicate and often dangerous dance of courtly life. For Marie, the transition from the Habsburg court of Vienna to the opulent halls of Versailles was both exhilarating and intimidating. She would need to navigate this complex social labyrinth with care, as every gesture, every word, and every alliance could have profound implications.

The very architecture of Versailles was a testament to the power dynamics at play. The grand salons and intimate chambers were designed not just for comfort and beauty, but for spectacle and surveillance. Every room was filled with courtiers, each vying for attention, favor, and power, and Marie quickly learned that the eyes of the court were always upon her. Each day began with the ritual of the "lever," where she would be awoken in public view, surrounded by nobles who would witness her morning routine. This was not merely a matter of custom; it was a calculated performance that established her status as queen. The presence of courtiers during such intimate moments reinforced the ever-present scrutiny she faced.

Dining at Versailles was another arena of courtly life where social hierarchies were meticulously observed. Meals were elaborate affairs, characterized by ostentation and excess. The queen's table was a spectacle in itself, with lavish displays of food representing the wealth of the monarchy. However, the seating arrangements at these banquets were laden with political significance. Allies were seated close, while rivals were kept at a distance. Marie, who had been raised to prioritize family loyalty and diplomacy, found herself needing to master this new language of social maneuvering. She quickly discovered that a misplaced glance or an uninvited guest could spark rumors or cause rifts between powerful factions.

The intrigues of Versailles were further complicated by the presence of powerful figures such as the formidable Madame de Pompadour, the chief mistress of King Louis XV. The history of their relationship had left its imprint on the court, and Marie was acutely aware of the implications of her predecessor's influence. Madame de Pompadour, who had successfully navigated the treacherous waters of Versailles, had established herself as a patroness of the arts and an advisor to the king. Marie recognized that to thrive at court, she would need to cultivate her own relationships and carve out her own identity, separate from the shadows cast by those who had come before her.

As Marie settled into her role, she encountered the intricate web of alliances and enmities that characterized court life. One of the most notable rivals was the Duchess of Bourbon, who had ambitions of her own and was not shy about expressing her disdain for the young queen. The Duchess, among others, would often whisper slights and rumors under their breath, casting a pall over Marie's attempts to gain acceptance. The queen's foreign origins became a point of contention, with many viewing her as an outsider in a land steeped in a rich and storied tradition. This only fueled her desire to assert herself, to demonstrate that she could embody the spirit of French royalty despite her Austrian heritage.

In this environment, Marie's social skills became paramount. She learned to engage in the art of conversation, to compliment and flatter those around her, and to deflect criticisms with grace and charm. Yet, the court's subtleties often left her feeling isolated. She would find solace in forming friendships with a select group of companions, including the charming and witty countess, Madame de Polignac. These alliances provided her with a support system amidst the backstabbing and gossip, but they also exposed her to the risks of loyalty. The very act of befriending someone could lead to suspicions and enhance the rumors swirling about her.

Fashion played a critical role in the intricate dance of court life, serving as both a tool of self-expression and a weapon in social warfare. Marie, already known for her beauty, quickly became a fashion icon, heralding a new era of style that prioritized extravagance and luxury. Her gowns, adorned with intricate embroidery and lavish fabrics, became the talk of the court. However, her sartorial choices also drew ire. Critics claimed she was out of touch with the struggles of the common people, and her opulent wardrobe became synonymous with the excesses of monarchy during a time of economic hardship for France.

Understanding the importance of appearances, Marie carefully navigated these challenges, often opting for simpler attire during public appearances to quell the growing unrest among the populace. Yet the fabric of her identity remained tightly woven into the lavishness of her surroundings, and she found herself torn between the expectations of her role as queen and her desire to connect with her subjects.

As tensions brewed outside the gilded gates of Versailles, Marie learned that the court was a reflection of the kingdom's complexities. The alliances forged within its walls and the rivalries that simmered beneath the surface were not just personal but political. The queen was a pawn in a game far larger than herself, and she began to grasp that her role was not merely ceremonial; it was deeply entwined with the fate of France.

In her quest to navigate this world of luxury and ambition, Marie Antoinette found herself at a crossroads. The opulence of Versailles promised wealth and prestige, but it came at the cost of personal freedom and emotional connection. As she adjusted to her new life, she would need to balance the expectations placed upon her with her own desires and aspirations. The intricacies of court life would demand all of her cunning and resilience as she sought to carve a path through the complexities of power, loyalty, and the ever-watchful eyes of the court.

As Marie Antoinette settled into her new role at the court of Versailles, she quickly learned that life in this grand palace was as much about navigating the treacherous waters of personal relationships as it was about fulfilling her duties as queen. The opulence of the surroundings belied the underlying tensions that simmered among the courtiers, and Marie, a young girl from the Habsburg dynasty, found herself at the center of a complex web of struggles and rivalries.

From the moment she arrived in France, Marie Antoinette was thrust into a world where allegiances shifted like the seasons. The French court was notorious for its intricate hierarchy, where titles and lineage dictated one's status. Marie, as the new queen, was expected to command respect, yet her foreign origins made her a target for suspicion and resentment. Many courtiers viewed her with skepticism, questioning her loyalty and suitability to rule alongside Louis XVI. The whispers began almost immediately, as factions formed, each vying for influence over the young queen.

One of her most prominent rivals was the Duchess of Polignac, who initially welcomed Marie with open arms. The Duchess, seeking to secure her own position, endeared herself to the queen and became a close confidante. However, as Marie's favor at court grew, so too did the animosity from those who felt overshadowed by her presence. The Duchess's support came with strings attached, and Marie soon realized that her closest allies could also be her most dangerous adversaries. As the court's dynamics shifted, the once-supportive relationship between Marie and the Duchess became fraught with jealousy and competition.

The rivalry did not stop there. Marie's public persona as a fashionable, extravagant queen clashed with the austere expectations of the French people and nobility alike. She was seen as frivolous and disconnected from the needs of her subjects, particularly as France faced mounting financial troubles. The lavish parties and opulent gowns that characterized her reign drew sharp criticism, leading to a growing divide between the monarchy and the populace. Courtiers who once celebrated her style began to use her excesses as ammunition against her, fueling a narrative that portrayed her as a symbol of royal excess.

The emergence of the pamphlet wars during these years exacerbated the tensions. Pamphlets circulated throughout Paris, filled with scandalous rumors and vicious caricatures of the queen. These publications depicted her as a spendthrift, obsessed with luxury and indifferent to the plight of her people. The court was abuzz with gossip, and the queen found herself the subject of malicious stories that painted her as a foreign interloper more concerned with fashion than governance. Marie's attempts to defend herself were often undermined by the very people she sought to impress. Each misstep was exploited, and she soon learned that trust was a scarce commodity in the palace.

Among the courtiers, the rivalry extended beyond mere jealousy; it was also a reflection of the broader political landscape. Marie's marriage to Louis XVI was part of a strategic alliance between France and Austria, and this connection was a constant source of conflict. The French aristocracy often viewed her with suspicion, believing that her Austrian heritage made her incapable of truly understanding French interests. The growing discontent with the monarchy was palpable, and courtiers began to question Marie's influence over her husband. Some whispered that she was leading him astray, encouraging his more extravagant tendencies and distancing him from the governance of the country.

As these rivalries intensified, Marie Antoinette found herself increasingly isolated. The friendships she had hoped to cultivate often turned into battlegrounds of manipulation and betrayal. When she attempted to connect with other women of the court, she encountered a landscape fraught with competition for favor. The court was a theater of social politics, and Marie had to learn quickly how to navigate the delicate balance between friendship and rivalry. Even her efforts to form alliances with other influential women were met with skepticism, as many viewed her as an outsider unworthy of their trust.

Amidst the struggles, Marie also grappled with her own insecurities. The weight of expectation rested heavily on her shoulders; as queen, she was tasked with producing an heir and securing the future of the Bourbon dynasty. The pressure to conform to traditional roles while remaining true to herself was daunting. She often found solace in her friendships with women who shared her interests, such as the Duchesse de Polignac, but these relationships could be as volatile as they were comforting.

The queen's attempts to assert her authority were frequently met with resistance. Court meetings, where decisions were made and alliances forged, became arenas of contention. She struggled to be taken seriously in discussions dominated by men, many of whom resented her influence over the king. Marie's efforts to engage in political discourse were often dismissed, reinforcing her feelings of inadequacy and isolation. She had arrived in France as a young girl filled with dreams of grandeur, but the reality of court life soon proved to be a trial by fire.

Despite the challenges she faced, Marie did not succumb to despair. Instead, she began to develop her strategies for survival. She learned to identify allies and enemies, often playing courtiers against one another to secure her position. Her charm and intelligence became her weapons, and she cultivated a reputation as a queen who was capable of both warmth and cunning. Marie Antoinette's ability to adapt in the face of adversity became one of her defining traits, even as the pressures of court life continued to mount.

In navigating the labyrinth of rivalries and struggles, Marie Antoinette's character began to crystallize. She was no longer just the naïve archduchess from Austria; she was evolving into a queen who would learn the art of diplomacy, the importance of alliances, and the necessity of self-preservation in a world rife with intrigue. The lessons she garnered from her tumultuous relationships at Versailles would shape her future decisions and ultimately influence the course of her reign. As she contended with the myriad of challenges presented by those around her, Marie began to understand that power at court was as much about perception as it was about reality—a lesson that would serve her well in the tumultuous years to come.

As Marie Antoinette settled into her new life at the opulent court of Versailles, she soon realized that survival in this glittering world required more than just a royal title and a stunning wardrobe. The intricate web of alliances and friendships she would weave was essential to her success as queen. In a court so teeming with ambition, envy, and intrigue, the relationships she cultivated would provide her with both support and protection amid the growing tensions of her reign.

Initially, Marie Antoinette's position as the Austrian archduchess was a double-edged sword. While her marriage to Louis XVI had been celebrated as a symbol of Franco-Austrian unity, the perception of her as a foreigner was a constant source of scrutiny. The French court, with its long-standing customs and traditions, was not easily swayed by her charms. The courtiers regarded her with a mixture of suspicion and disdain, often referring to her as "l'Autrichienne"—the Austrian. To navigate this precarious environment, she understood that she needed allies who could help her gain acceptance and influence.

Among her earliest supporters was the Duchess of Polignac, a woman of considerable charm and social standing, who became one of Marie Antoinette's closest confidantes. Their friendship blossomed quickly, and the duchess became a vital source of advice and companionship in the often lonely and isolating atmosphere of the court. Polignac's loyalty was unwavering, and she helped Marie Antoinette to connect with other influential figures, facilitating her integration into the court's social fabric. Together, they attended balls and lavish gatherings, where the queen's vibrant personality began to shine, captivating those around her.

Marie Antoinette also recognized the importance of building relationships with the king's family. Initially, she made efforts to bond with Louis XVI's siblings, particularly Madame Élisabeth, who was known for her piety and devotion to her brother. Their shared commitment to family and duty created a foundation for mutual respect. However, the queen's exuberance and lifestyle often clashed with the more austere values upheld by the royal family. Nevertheless, she managed to maintain cordial relationships, often inviting them to her private soirées at the Petit Trianon, where she could express herself more freely away from the formalities of the main court.

The queen's social calendar became a tapestry of alliances, each thread carefully woven to secure her position. She hosted extravagant gatherings, where the laughter and music echoed through the halls of her private retreat. These events became legendary, showcasing the queen's flair for entertainment and her desire to foster a sense of camaraderie among her guests. Through these gatherings, she not only entertained but also strategically aligned herself with powerful noble families, each relationship serving to solidify her status and influence.

However, the court was also a place of fierce rivalries. The competition for favor was relentless, and Marie Antoinette quickly learned that not all friendships were genuine. One of her most notable adversaries was the formidable Madame de Maintenon, who had previously been a favorite of Louis XIV. Though past her prime, de Maintenon wielded significant influence and was determined to maintain her relevance in court politics. The queen's open displays of affection for her own favorites often incited envy, leading to whispers and gossip that would follow her like a shadow. To counteract this animosity, Marie Antoinette engaged in a careful balancing act, ensuring that she remained on good terms with those who might threaten her position.

As time passed, Marie Antoinette's efforts to build alliances bore fruit. She became a central figure in the court, adored by many for her vivacity and generosity. She was often seen at the gardens of Versailles, engaging in playful activities with her courtiers, promoting a sense of unity that contrasted sharply with the political turmoil brewing outside the palace walls. Her ability to navigate the complexities of court life was a testament to her resilience and adaptability.

Despite these successes, the queen's friendships were not without their challenges. The political landscape of France was shifting, and her foreign heritage continued to be a point of contention. The burgeoning discontent among the populace, exacerbated by financial strife and political unrest, seeped into the very walls of Versailles. As rumors circulated and tensions escalated, the friendships she had nurtured began to fracture under pressure.

The arrival of the Revolution only intensified the existing rivalries within the court. Allies became adversaries, and the atmosphere of camaraderie that Marie Antoinette had cultivated began to disintegrate. Some of her closest friends were implicated in political scandals, while others turned away as they sought self-preservation amidst the chaos. The betrayal of those she once trusted was perhaps the most painful aspect of her adjustment to the realities of being queen.

As the storms of revolution gathered, Marie Antoinette was forced to confront the consequences of her alliances. The friendships she had built, once a source of strength, became fraught with danger. Yet, amid the turmoil, she remained steadfast, holding onto the bonds that had sustained her through the challenges of court life. Even as the world around her began to crumble, she continued to nurture those relationships, finding solace in the faces of the few loyal friends who stood by her side.

In the grand tapestry of Marie Antoinette's life at Versailles, the friendships and alliances she forged were both a source of joy and a means of survival. Her ability to connect with others, to navigate the treacherous waters of court politics, marked her reign with moments of brilliance even as shadows loomed ever closer. These relationships, filled with both warmth and rivalry, would ultimately shape the narrative of her tragic journey as queen of France, leaving an indelible mark on her legacy.

Chapter 4: Queen of France: The Rise of Marie Antoinette

Marie Antoinette's coronation as Queen of France was not merely a ceremonial event; it was a moment steeped in the complexities of statecraft, personal ambition, and the weight of public expectation. On May 7, 1775, she stood in the hallowed halls of Reims Cathedral, surrounded by opulent decorations and a throng of onlookers, both noble and common. The air was thick with anticipation, and her heart raced with the gravity of the role she was about to assume.

The processional that led her to the cathedral was an extravagant affair. Carriages adorned with lush fabrics and gilded embellishments rolled through the streets of Reims, a visual feast that showcased the wealth and power of the French monarchy. Marie, dressed in a sumptuous gown of golden silk, felt the eyes of the crowd upon her. They lined the streets, a sea of faces filled with awe, envy, and expectation. This was the moment when she would transform from the Austrian archduchess into the absolute Queen of France—a title that came with both privilege and peril.

As she entered the cathedral, the atmosphere shifted. The high ceilings echoed with the solemnity of the occasion, and the flickering candlelight created an ethereal glow around her. The ceremony was steeped in centuries of tradition, and every gesture held significance. She knelt before the altar, her heart pounding as she was anointed with holy oil—a symbolic act that not only marked her as the divine ruler but also bound her to her people in a sacred covenant. The Archbishop of Reims, his voice resonant and commanding, recited prayers and blessings, urging the heavens to guide and protect the new queen.

Yet, the magnificence of her coronation belied the challenges that lay ahead. Although Marie Antoinette had arrived in France under the auspices of creating a political alliance, the reality of her position was far more complicated. She was expected to embody the virtues of the French monarchy, to be not only a figurehead but a beloved mother of the nation. However, she was also a foreigner in a land where suspicion and resentment simmered just beneath the surface. Her marriage to Louis XVI was meant to solidify ties between Austria and France, yet it also brought with it a burden of scrutiny and skepticism.

As she took her place on the throne beside Louis, the grandeur of the moment was punctuated by the struggles that characterized their marriage. Louis was a reluctant king, often indecisive and overshadowed by the weight of his responsibilities. Marie, with her vivacious spirit, sought to invigorate the court and bring life into their reign. Yet, the couple's personal dynamics were often overshadowed by the broader political landscape. Their inability to produce an heir in the early years of their marriage only added to the tension, fueling rumors and gossip that danced through the corridors of Versailles.

Despite these challenges, Marie Antoinette's coronation marked the beginning of her ascent into a world of influence and visibility. With the title of queen came opportunities to shape cultural and social norms within the court. She was not merely a passive figure; she sought to redefine the role of the queen, stepping beyond traditional expectations. In the months following her coronation, she began to host lavish gatherings, transforming the court's social fabric with her personal flair.

Marie Antoinette was acutely aware that to win the hearts of the French people, she had to engage with them on a personal level. The opulence of her coronation was followed by a series of public appearances where she showcased her charm and vivacity. She became a trendsetter, popularizing extravagant fashion and extravagant hairstyles that captured the imagination of the public. The Petit Trianon, a retreat she established on the grounds of Versailles, became a symbol of her desire for a more relatable monarchy. Here, she could escape the rigid protocols of court life and embrace a more informal, pastoral existence, often entertaining friends and confidants in a setting that felt more personal than regal.

However, the rise of Marie Antoinette was not without its pitfalls. The wealth and extravagance that followed her ascension became focal points for criticism, especially as the country faced mounting financial turmoil. The disparity between the opulence of the court and the struggles of the common people grew increasingly pronounced. Critics began to question the morality of a queen who indulged in luxury while her subjects faced hardship. The whispers of discontent that had once been mere murmurs began to swell into a chorus of outrage.

Marie Antoinette was often portrayed in the press as the epitome of excess, her every indulgence scrutinized and exaggerated. The infamous phrase "Let them eat cake," attributed to her during a time of famine, exemplified her perceived disconnect from the realities of her people, though there is little historical evidence to support that she ever uttered those words. The press and public opinion began to paint her not just as a queen but as a symbol of everything wrong with the monarchy.

As her reign progressed, the tension between her desire for personal expression and the responsibilities of her role as queen became ever more pronounced. The initial excitement of her coronation faded into the complexities of governance, where her foreign origins and lavish lifestyle were increasingly viewed with suspicion. Despite this, Marie Antoinette remained determined to carve out her own identity within the confines of her royal role, striving to balance the expectations of her position with her own aspirations and desires.

In the years following her coronation, Marie Antoinette would face trials that would test her resolve and redefine her legacy. The ascension that once promised a new era of stability and prosperity for France would soon be overshadowed by the political upheaval that lay ahead, but in that moment of coronation, she was poised at the pinnacle of power, ready to embrace the challenges of her new life as the queen. The road ahead would be fraught with obstacles, but her spirit and determination would guide her through the tumultuous times to come.

As Marie Antoinette settled into her role as Queen of France, the contours of her influence began to take shape within the gilded halls of Versailles. The young queen, who had once been a foreign archduchess, was now tasked with embodying the spirit and values of the French monarchy. Her position, while immensely powerful, was fraught with the complexities of court politics, public perception, and the expectations of her role.

Marie Antoinette's ascent to power was marked by her ability to navigate the intricacies of court life, where alliances were forged and rivalries simmered beneath the surface. She understood early on that her influence extended beyond mere ceremonial duties; it encompassed the ability to sway opinions, garner support, and even direct the course of political events. Her charm and vivacity drew people to her, and she quickly became a focal point of the court. She was not merely a figurehead; she was a queen who had the potential to shape the narrative of her reign.

One of the most significant aspects of her influence was her relationship with her husband, King Louis XVI. Although their marriage had initially been seen as a political alliance intended to strengthen ties between France and Austria, it gradually evolved into a partnership that allowed Marie Antoinette to exert her influence more directly. The king, known for his indecisiveness, often relied on her counsel, especially in matters concerning the court and public image. Marie Antoinette's ability to present herself as a competent and compassionate queen helped to bolster Louis's authority, even if he often appeared overshadowed by his wife's charisma.

Marie Antoinette also understood the importance of public perception in solidifying her power. She adeptly managed her image, portraying herself as both a devoted wife and a benevolent queen. She engaged in charitable endeavors, supporting various causes and demonstrating a genuine interest in the welfare of her subjects. By hosting lavish events that showcased her generosity, she sought to win the hearts of the French people, many of whom were captivated by her beauty and grace. This carefully curated public persona was not just a façade but a strategic maneuver that allowed her to cultivate loyalty among the nobility and the populace.

The queen's influence was further amplified through her patronage of the arts and culture. She recognized the power of art as a means of shaping public opinion and reinforcing her status. Marie Antoinette became a patron of artists, musicians, and writers, fostering an environment that celebrated creativity and innovation. Her support helped usher in a cultural renaissance at Versailles, where the arts thrived under her guidance. The queen's preference for theatricality and extravagance influenced fashion and design, setting trends that rippled through society. Her iconic style became synonymous with the height of elegance, and she was often credited with transforming the aesthetic landscape of her time.

However, Marie Antoinette's rise was not without its challenges. The very qualities that endeared her to some also fueled the ire of others. Her opulent lifestyle and the extravagant expenditures of the royal court became points of contention amid the growing discontent among the French populace. Critics accused her of being out of touch with the struggles faced by ordinary citizens, particularly in the face of rising bread prices and economic instability. The infamous phrase "Let them eat cake," often attributed to her, epitomized the disconnect perceived by many between the queen's lavish lifestyle and the harsh realities endured by the lower classes, though it is widely debated whether she ever uttered those words.

In the face of mounting criticism, Marie Antoinette adapted her approach, striving to mitigate the backlash against her. She sought to engage more actively with the people, participating in public ceremonies and charitable initiatives. She even took to the streets during crises, demonstrating a willingness to be seen among her subjects. This shift in strategy was indicative of her understanding of the delicate balance between royal privilege and public duty. She recognized that her power was not merely derived from her title, but also from her ability to connect with the people of France.

Despite her efforts, the political landscape shifted dramatically in the years leading up to the revolution. The queen's influence began to wane as the socio-political climate became increasingly volatile. The financial crisis gripping France was exacerbated by years of mismanagement and an inequitable tax system that burdened the lower classes while preserving the privileges of the aristocracy. The growing discontent culminated in calls for reform, and Marie Antoinette found herself at the center of a storm of criticism as a symbol of the excesses of the monarchy.

In this tumultuous environment, Marie Antoinette's power became increasingly precarious. Her earlier attempts to assert her influence were overshadowed by the rising tide of revolutionary fervor. The queen's past extravagances were scrutinized, and her image transformed from that of a beloved royal to a target of resentment. The very qualities that had once endeared her to the court now became sources of scandal and derision.

As the revolution gained momentum, Marie Antoinette's role shifted from one of influence to one of survival. The queen who had once wielded power from the opulent halls of Versailles now faced the very real threat of losing everything she had known. The revolutionaries painted her as a foreign interloper, a traitor to the French people, and her attempts to navigate this treacherous new reality would ultimately determine her fate.

In retrospect, Marie Antoinette's influence and power were emblematic of the complexities of monarchy in an era poised on the brink of monumental change. Her life encapsulated the dualities of privilege and vulnerability, love and disdain, extravagance and tragedy. As her reign progressed, the delicate balance she sought to maintain between the crown and the people unraveled, leading to a dramatic fall from grace that would define her legacy in the annals of history.

As Marie Antoinette settled into her role as the Queen of France, her responsibilities within the royal household began to crystallize, transforming her from a foreign bride into a central figure of the French monarchy. The royal household was a complex institution, steeped in tradition and expectation, and it fell to the queen to navigate these intricate waters while projecting an image of power and grace.

The structure of the royal household was both grand and elaborate, reflecting the opulence of the French crown. It encompassed a vast array of officials, courtiers, and servants, each with their own designated roles and responsibilities. At the helm was the Grand Master of the Household, responsible for the overall management and organization, but it was the queen who ultimately dictated the tone and atmosphere of her court. Marie Antoinette had to become a master of both the ceremonial and the practical, a balancing act that required keen political instincts and an understanding of the delicate dynamics of power.

One of her primary duties was to preside over the daily court rituals, which were laden with symbolism and importance. The morning ritual, known as the "lever," was a public affair that allowed courtiers to pay their respects and seek favor. Marie Antoinette would arise in the presence of her ladies-in-waiting, dressed in sumptuous gowns that showcased her status and personal style. This ritual was not merely a matter of vanity; it was an essential part of her role as queen, reinforcing her position and allowing her to maintain visibility at court.

Throughout the day, the queen was expected to engage with her ladies and courtiers, participating in various activities that ranged from needlework to music and dance. These gatherings were not only social events but also opportunities for political maneuvering. Courtiers sought to gain Marie Antoinette's favor and influence, subtly vying for her attention and support. The queen, in turn, learned to navigate these relationships carefully, recognizing that alliances formed within the court could shape her influence over policy and governance.

Marie Antoinette's household was marked by a unique blend of personal preference and tradition. She surrounded herself with a circle of trusted companions, many of whom were drawn from her native Austria. This strategy served a dual purpose: it provided her with a sense of familiarity and comfort while simultaneously reinforcing her position as a foreign queen in a nation that remained wary of her origins. Notably, her closest confidante, the Duchess de Polignac, became a significant presence in her life, offering both companionship and political savvy as they maneuvered through the complexities of court life.

As queen, Marie Antoinette also held the responsibility of overseeing the royal finances related to her household. The expenses incurred by the court were vast, and her lavish tastes often drew scrutiny from both the public and the nobility. The queen's penchant for extravagant gowns, exquisite jewelry, and sumptuous banquets became a focal point of criticism, particularly during a time when France was grappling with economic instability. She was acutely aware of the fine line between displaying the magnificence of the crown and the potential backlash from a populace struggling to make ends meet.

In addition to her ceremonial duties, Marie Antoinette was expected to fulfill her role as a mother. The queen was responsible for the upbringing of her children, a task that required her to balance her obligations to her family with the demands of the court. Her approach to motherhood was often scrutinized, as the public had high expectations of her maternal instincts. Marie Antoinette, however, was determined to provide a nurturing environment while also embracing the traditional role of a queen. She fostered a close bond with her children, especially with her eldest daughter, Madame Royale, preparing her for the eventual responsibilities of royal life.

The queen's duties extended beyond mere appearances and motherhood; she was also involved in charitable endeavors, which were essential for maintaining her image and the monarchy's reputation. Marie Antoinette supported various charitable institutions, including hospitals and orphanages, which allowed her to cultivate a more favorable public image amidst growing discontent. Her involvement in these initiatives demonstrated a desire to connect with the people, even as her extravagant lifestyle often contradicted her intentions.

As the years progressed, the political landscape of France began to shift dramatically, and the role of the queen became increasingly precarious. The tensions between the monarchy and the burgeoning revolutionary sentiment posed a significant challenge to Marie Antoinette's reign. While she remained committed to her duties, the environment at court grew more volatile, and the expectations placed upon her evolved. The queen was not only a figurehead but also a target for dissent and hostility, as the public began to blame her for the nation's economic woes.

Throughout the tumultuous years of her reign, Marie Antoinette navigated the complexities of her royal duties with a combination of grace and defiance. She embraced the pomp and circumstance of her position, all while struggling to reconcile her personal desires with the demands of her role. Her ability to adapt to the shifting tides of court life showcased her resilience, but it also underscored the inherent challenges of being a queen in a time of crisis.

In the end, Marie Antoinette's tenure as queen was defined by her quest for identity within a rigid framework of expectation. The royal household was not merely a backdrop to her life; it was a living, breathing entity that shaped her experiences and the legacy she would leave behind. As she faced the trials of her reign, she would come to embody the complexities of a monarchy on the brink of collapse, leaving an indelible mark on history as both a symbol of luxury and a victim of scandal and tragedy.

Chapter 5: Indulgence and Extravagance: The Height of Luxury

Marie Antoinette's reign as queen was synonymous with opulence, and no aspect of her life epitomized this better than her beloved Petit Trianon. Nestled within the vast grounds of the Palace of Versailles, this charming retreat offered a respite from the rigid protocols of court life, allowing the queen to indulge her extravagant tastes while simultaneously crafting a more personal, intimate atmosphere. The Petit Trianon was not just a residence; it was a manifestation of her aspirations, a sanctuary where the queen could escape the weight of her royal obligations and revel in the joys of leisure.

Constructed in the mid-18th century under the orders of King Louis XV, the Petit Trianon was designed by architect Ange-Jacques Gabriel. It was initially intended as a gift for Madame de Pompadour, but upon her death, it became the favored retreat of Marie Antoinette after her marriage in 1770. The queen transformed the estate into a haven that reflected her personality and passions, infusing it with a distinctive style that celebrated simplicity and nature, a stark contrast to the grandeur of Versailles.

Upon entering the Petit Trianon, visitors were greeted by the harmonious blend of nature and architecture. Surrounded by lush gardens and serene landscapes, the building itself showcased elegant neoclassical design, with its pale stone façade and gracefully proportioned interiors. The queen's influence was evident in every detail, from the exquisite furnishings to the delicate tapestries that adorned its walls. Each room conveyed an air of intimacy, as though the queen had personally curated an environment that spoke to her innermost desires and sentiments.

Marie Antoinette's vision for the Petit Trianon extended beyond mere aesthetics. She saw it as a place for leisure and amusement, a sanctuary where she could gather her closest friends for lavish parties and extravagant gatherings. The queen's penchant for lavish celebrations was legendary, and the Petit Trianon became a stage for some of the most opulent events of her reign. These soirées were characterized by a carefree spirit and a sense of intimacy that was often absent from the formal court events at Versailles.

The gardens surrounding the Petit Trianon were meticulously designed, offering an idyllic backdrop for outdoor festivities. The queen hosted picnics, theatrical performances, and masquerade balls that drew the elite of French society. On warm summer evenings, the air resonated with laughter and music as guests reveled in the freedom that the estate provided. The queen, dressed in the latest fashions, would lead her guests in dances that echoed the joyous abandon of youth. The opulence of these gatherings was matched only by the sheer delight of their informality.

One of the most memorable events held at the Petit Trianon was the fête de la Nouvelle France in 1774, which celebrated the queen's recent ascension to the throne. This extravagant affair transformed the estate into a fantastical representation of the New World, complete with exotic decorations and sumptuous feasts. Guests were treated to theatrical performances that depicted colonial life, immersing themselves in a world far removed from the political turmoil brewing outside the palace walls. The lavishness of the fête underscored Marie Antoinette's desire to project an image of prosperity and vitality, even as France faced mounting economic challenges.

Yet, amidst the grandeur of her parties, the queen faced growing criticism. Her lavish lifestyle, particularly the opulence of the Petit Trianon, became a focal point for the discontent brewing among the French populace. While Marie Antoinette reveled in her role as queen, hosting grand celebrations and surrounding herself with luxury, the stark realities of the country's financial struggles could not be ignored. The growing rift between the monarchy and the people was exacerbated by tales of excess that circulated through the salons and streets of Paris. For many, the Petit Trianon embodied the excesses of the monarchy, a stark contrast to the struggles of the common people.

In response to the mounting criticism, Marie Antoinette attempted to recalibrate her public image. She sought to portray herself as a devoted mother and a benevolent queen, engaging in charitable works and establishing connections with the less fortunate. However, the lavish parties at the Petit Trianon continued to draw scrutiny. The queen's attempts to distance herself from the excesses of her life often fell flat, as her extravagant soirées overshadowed her more modest endeavors.

The queen's obsession with fashion also played a significant role in the culture of indulgence that surrounded her. Marie Antoinette became a fashion icon, setting trends with her elaborate gowns and intricate hairstyles. Each party at the Petit Trianon was an opportunity for her to showcase the latest styles, often designed by the renowned dressmaker Rose Bertin. The queen's outfits were as much a part of the spectacle as the parties themselves, and her fashion choices were scrutinized by both admirers and critics alike. While she basked in the admiration of the court, the extravagant expenses incurred by her wardrobe contributed to the perception of her as out of touch with the realities facing her subjects.

As the revolution loomed on the horizon, the Petit Trianon, once a symbol of Marie Antoinette's indulgent lifestyle, became a bittersweet reminder of her lost freedom and the fading opulence of the monarchy. The estate, which had once been a sanctuary of joy and escapism, would soon fall silent as the world outside descended into chaos. The lavish parties, once a testament to her status and power, would become relics of a bygone era, overshadowed by the stark realities of revolution and change.

Marie Antoinette's time at the Petit Trianon encapsulated the dualities of her life — the exquisite beauty of luxury intertwined with the impending tragedy of her fate. The estate serves as a poignant reminder of her complexities: a queen who sought refuge in indulgence while the world around her spiraled into turmoil. As the revolution unfurled its wrath, the Petit Trianon stood witness to the profound transformations that would forever alter the landscape of France, reflecting the contradictions of a life steeped in both privilege and impending doom.

As Marie Antoinette settled into her role as Queen of France, her influence extended far beyond the political realm and into the fabric of French culture, particularly in the realm of fashion. With a keen eye for aesthetics and a desire to express her individuality, she quickly became the epitome of style at the opulent court of Versailles. Her wardrobe, a reflection of her personality and status, would ultimately elevate her to the status of a fashion icon, revered and emulated by women across Europe.

Marie Antoinette's journey into the world of fashion began with her royal upbringing in the Habsburg court, where she was accustomed to the grandeur and elegance that accompanied her status. However, it was at Versailles that her taste would blossom into a distinctive and influential style that would leave an indelible mark on the fashion landscape of the 18th century. She was not merely a passive consumer of fashion; rather, she was an innovator who embraced the changing tides of sartorial preferences and popularized them through her own choices.

One of the defining aspects of Marie Antoinette's fashion was her ability to blend traditional court attire with more relaxed and playful elements. Her early years in France saw her wearing the elaborate gowns typical of royalty, characterized by sumptuous fabrics, extravagant embroidery, and towering hairstyles. However, as she grew more comfortable in her role, she began to favor lighter, more whimsical designs that reflected her personality and the changing tastes of the era. The extravagant panniers of earlier years, which had created an exaggerated silhouette, gradually gave way to softer lines and more natural forms, as she embraced the Rococo style that was taking Europe by storm.

Marie Antoinette's most iconic fashion statement was perhaps her love for the "chemise à la reine," a simple, flowing white gown that she first donned in the late 1780s. This garment, which resembled a loose-fitting chemise, was a radical departure from the rigid structures of court fashion, signifying both comfort and a deliberate move away from the ostentation that characterized the French court. When she wore this gown, it raised eyebrows and sparked controversy among her contemporaries, particularly those who viewed it as a sign of her disregard for royal decorum. Nevertheless, the dress became emblematic of her style and a symbol of her desire to break free from the oppressive constraints of royal fashion norms.

Her penchant for fashion also extended to accessories, with Marie Antoinette often adorning herself with extravagant jewelry that sparkled against her sumptuous gowns. From exquisite diamond necklaces to elaborate tiaras, each piece was chosen with the intention of both enhancing her beauty and solidifying her status as the queen. She was known to collaborate with renowned jewelers, commissioning pieces that would not only captivate but also set trends. The famous diamond necklace, although mired in scandal, is one such example of her extravagant taste, illustrating the lengths to which she would go to embrace the allure of luxury.

The Queen's influence on fashion was not limited to her personal choices; she also played a significant role in shaping the French textile industry. With her interest in innovative fabrics and designs, Marie Antoinette became a patron of French artisans and manufacturers. She favored silk and fine textiles, leading to an increased demand for high-quality materials, which in turn spurred the local economy. Her preference for French craftsmanship over imported goods was a political statement in itself, signaling her commitment to the nation and its production capabilities. This emphasis on national pride in fashion resonated deeply with the populace and reinforced her position as a beloved figure, at least among the bourgeoisie and aristocracy.

However, her extravagant style was not without its critics. As France faced mounting financial difficulties, the extravagant fashions and lifestyles of the royal family, particularly that of Marie Antoinette, fueled public resentment. The Queen's lavish parties, the opulence of her wardrobe, and her seemingly carefree attitude towards the plight of the common people became fodder for political propaganda. The phrase, "Let them eat cake," often attributed to her, although likely apocryphal, encapsulated the perception that the Queen was disconnected from the realities of her subjects. This perception was exacerbated by her penchant for displaying her luxurious lifestyle in stark contrast to the suffering of the French populace.

Yet, through it all, Marie Antoinette remained a steadfast figure in the world of fashion, confident in her choices and unafraid to express herself. The Queen's style was not just about clothing; it was about identity. She used fashion as a means of asserting her individuality in a court that often sought to dictate behavior and presentation. Her bold choices often reflected her evolving self-image, as she navigated the complexities of her role as a foreign queen in a country rife with political turmoil.

Even in her later years, as the winds of revolution began to sweep through France, her impact on fashion remained undeniable. Her legacy as a fashion icon would continue long after her execution, influencing generations of designers and fashionistas. The romanticized image of Marie Antoinette, bedecked in luxurious gowns and extravagant jewels, would become a touchstone for idealized femininity in the centuries that followed.

In the world of fashion, Marie Antoinette's life serves as a paradox – a celebration of beauty and style, intertwined with the very tragedies that would ultimately lead to her downfall. As she walked the gilded halls of Versailles, adorned in the finest silks and shimmering jewels, she embodied a complex interplay of luxury, scandal, and the stark reality of a nation on the brink of revolution. Her story is not merely one of opulence but also a poignant reminder of the perils of excess and the fleeting nature of fame and fortune.

As Marie Antoinette settled into her role as the Queen of France, she quickly became synonymous with extravagance and indulgence, drawing both admiration and sharp criticism from various quarters. The opulence of her lifestyle, juxtaposed against the backdrop of a nation in economic distress, would become a significant point of contention and a source of scandal that reverberated through the annals of history.

From her earliest days at Versailles, Marie was thrust into a world that celebrated luxury. The gilded halls of the palace echoed with laughter and music, and the air was thick with the scent of lavish banquets. Yet, while the Queen reveled in the splendor of her surroundings, the growing discontent among her subjects began to fester. Critics noted that the royal court was a realm detached from the struggles of ordinary French citizens, who were grappling with food shortages and rising taxes. The stark contrast between the lives of the nobility and the plight of the common people could not have been more pronounced.

Marie's penchant for grand festivities and extravagant spending became the focal point of public scrutiny. The Petit Trianon, a charming pleasure palace gifted to her by Louis XVI, became a symbol of her excesses. Here, she transformed into a pastoral queen, hosting elaborate soirées that featured sumptuous feasts and elaborate costumes. Guests were presented with culinary delights that would have fed entire villages, while the Queen dressed in the latest fashions, adorned with jewels that sparkled like stars. Such displays, while captivating to some, were seen as an affront to the suffering populace, who were well aware of the kingdom's dire financial state.

The criticism intensified with the notorious Diamond Necklace Affair, which would further tarnish her image. In 1785, a scandal broke involving a lavish necklace that had been commissioned by the late Madame de Pompadour. A group of con artists, exploiting the Queen's name, attempted to purchase the necklace under the pretense that Marie Antoinette herself had ordered it. When the scheme unraveled, the public was quick to associate the Queen with the scandal, further fueling the perception of her as a figure of excess and immorality. The affair was sensationalized by pamphleteers, many of whom disseminated vicious caricatures and distortions of her character, depicting her as a greedy and manipulative woman. This scandal not only embarrassed the monarchy but also became a rallying point for those who sought to undermine the royal family.

The Queen's critics were relentless, portraying her as the epitome of everything wrong with the monarchy. The phrase "Let them eat cake," which many attributed to her, became a symbol of her supposed indifference to the plight of the poor. Although historians largely agree that she never uttered these words, the idea persisted, showcasing the disconnect between Marie's luxurious lifestyle and the realities of her subjects. This narrative was perpetuated by political pamphlets that painted her as a foreigner who had betrayed her adopted country, further alienating her from the French populace.

As the revolution began to brew, Marie Antoinette's lifestyle was scrutinized with renewed vigor. Her extravagant spending became a focal point of revolutionary rhetoric, as the populace grew increasingly frustrated with the monarchy's apparent disregard for their suffering. The Court's penchant for lavish balls and extravagant fashions became fodder for revolutionary propaganda, depicting the royals as out-of-touch elites living in a bubble of luxury while their subjects starved.

In the face of such criticism, Marie's response was often to retreat further into her cocoon of opulence. She sought solace in her lavish lifestyle, believing that grand parties and beautiful silks could shield her from the growing discontent outside the gilded gates of Versailles. However, her refusal to acknowledge the changing tides only deepened the divide between her and the citizens of France. Her extravagant tastes, once celebrated, began to be viewed as a callous disregard for the welfare of the nation.

Even her attempts to reform her spending were met with skepticism. Although she made efforts to curtail her expenditures and support charitable causes, such gestures were often overshadowed by the ongoing spectacle of court life. The luxurious gowns and extravagant jewelry continued to draw the eye, and the public remained unconvinced that the Queen truly understood the hardships they faced.

As revolutionary fervor swept through France, Marie became a symbol of the monarchy's excesses. Her lifestyle was an easy target for revolutionaries who sought to dismantle the old regime. The very things that had once defined her reign—lavish parties, sumptuous feasts, and extravagant fashion—turned into weapons wielded against her. The more she attempted to retreat from public view, the more the narrative of the extravagant queen persisted, ultimately sealing her fate as the revolution gained momentum.

The irony of Marie Antoinette's life was that her desire for happiness and indulgence became her downfall. In her pursuit of a life filled with beauty and joy, she inadvertently alienated herself from the very people she was meant to serve. The opulence that once captivated the court turned into a symbol of her disconnect from reality. As the revolution progressed, the very fabric of her identity—woven with the threads of luxury and excess—was unraveled by the hands of those who had once admired her.

Marie Antoinette's life became a cautionary tale about the perils of excess and the importance of understanding the needs of the people. In the end, her story serves as a reminder of how the pursuit of personal pleasure, when divorced from empathy and responsibility, can lead to tragic consequences. As she faced the consequences of her choices, the echoes of her lavish lifestyle would resonate through history, forever marking her as a figure of scandal and tragedy—a queen who lived in luxury, but whose life ended in a tumult of public outrage and despair.

Chapter 6: The Seeds of Discontent: Political Turmoil

The financial crisis that gripped France in the late 18th century was not merely a consequence of poor management but rather the culmination of decades of extravagant spending, costly wars, and an inequitable taxation system. As the country teetered on the brink of bankruptcy, the effects rippled throughout society, from the opulent halls of Versailles to the impoverished streets of Paris, where the cries of the destitute were increasingly drowned out by the lavish banquets of the court.

Marie Antoinette, now accustomed to a life of luxury, found herself at the center of this tumultuous period. The extravagant lifestyle she was known for became a focal point of public disdain, as she was perceived not just as a queen but as a symbol of the excesses that had led the nation to its financial precipice. The Queen's public image, long crafted through elaborate displays of wealth and fashion, morphed into an emblem of everything that was wrong with the monarchy. Her critics, stoking the fires of discontent, painted her as a foreigner more interested in personal indulgence than in the plight of her adopted countrymen.

The financial turmoil was exacerbated by France's involvement in several costly wars, notably the American Revolutionary War. The decision to support the American colonies in their struggle for independence against Great Britain was initially seen as a noble cause, a way for France to regain prestige lost during the Seven Years' War. However, the financial burden it placed on the French treasury was immense. The government found itself deep in debt, and the king's attempts to raise funds through a series of tax reforms were met with resistance from the privileged classes, who were unwilling to relinquish their tax exemptions.

As the financial crisis deepened, Louis XVI, a well-meaning but indecisive king, called upon the Assembly of Notables in 1787 to address the dire state of the nation. Among those present were the noblemen and clergy, who were to provide counsel on how to restore the finances of the realm. What ensued was a spectacle of self-interest, as the privileged classes defended their own interests rather than consider the plight of the common people. The discussions were fruitless, and the Assembly ultimately refused to endorse the reforms proposed by the king, leaving him with no choice but to summon the Estates-General, a general assembly representing the three estates of the realm: the clergy, the nobility, and the common people.

The convening of the Estates-General in May 1789 marked a pivotal moment in French history. It had not been called for over a century, and the expectations were high. The Third Estate, representing the common people, was particularly vocal in its demands for reform. They were tired of bearing the brunt of taxation while the aristocracy and clergy enjoyed their privileges without accountability. The rift between the estates was palpable, and tensions simmered just beneath the surface.

Marie Antoinette, while closely tied to the monarchy, was also caught in the crosshairs of a rapidly changing political landscape. As the situation grew more precarious, her perceived frivolity became a weapon for those who sought to undermine the monarchy. The Queen's lavish spending habits were often exaggerated and reported in pamphlets and newspapers, further fueling public outrage. The infamous phrase attributed to her, "Let them eat cake," though likely apocryphal, encapsulated the growing disdain for her disconnect from the struggles of the masses. In reality, Marie Antoinette had worked to improve conditions for the poor, advocating for various charitable initiatives, yet these efforts were overshadowed by the prevailing narrative of excess.

The financial crisis reached a breaking point in the summer of 1789. The public was restless; bread prices soared, and famine loomed. The common people of Paris voiced their frustration through protests, and the atmosphere grew increasingly hostile towards the monarchy. On July 14, 1789, the storming of the Bastille became the spark that ignited the Revolution. What began as a desperate act of rebellion by the people seeking arms and ammunition quickly transformed into a symbol of the fight against tyranny and oppression.

In the wake of the Bastille's fall, the monarchy's power began to wane. The National Assembly, formed by the representatives of the Third Estate, began to draft reforms aimed at restructuring the government and addressing the grievances of the populace. The Queen, who had once been seen as a potential instrument of reconciliation, now found herself a target of the revolutionaries. Her status as a foreign queen only intensified the animosity, as many viewed her with suspicion and resentment, believing she held too much sway over her husband, the king.

The financial crisis, compounded by political turmoil and social unrest, had created an environment where the monarchy's legitimacy was increasingly questioned. The Queen's attempts to navigate this landscape were met with skepticism, as her previous indulgences became a source of ire rather than admiration. Her extravagant lifestyle, once a source of envy, became a poignant reminder of the vast chasm between the royal court and the suffering masses.

As the Revolution gained momentum, the monarchy's efforts to maintain power became desperate. Marie Antoinette's position as queen was precarious; she had to balance the royal prerogative with the demands of a society on the brink of transformation. The seeds of discontent sown by financial mismanagement were now bearing bitter fruit, and the very institution she represented was under siege. The Queen's life, once characterized by opulence and courtly intrigues, was now overshadowed by the specter of impending doom. As France spiraled into chaos, it became increasingly clear that the luxury and privilege enjoyed by the monarchy could no longer shield it from the reckoning that was to come.

As Marie Antoinette settled into her role as the Queen of France, she quickly became a focal point for both admiration and disdain among the populace and the political elite. The opulence of her lifestyle, juxtaposed against the growing discontent among the French people, made her a lightning rod for criticism. Amidst the political turmoil of the late 18th century, public perception of Marie Antoinette was shaped by a complex interplay of propaganda, societal expectations, and the rapid deterioration of France's economic stability.

At the heart of this perception was the stark contrast between the lavish lifestyle of the royal court and the harsh realities faced by the common people. As France grappled with crippling debt and rising food prices, the Queen's extravagant spending came under scrutiny. The lavish parties at the Petit Trianon, the extravagant gowns adorned with jewels, and the seemingly endless supply of luxury goods served as fodder for critics who painted her as out of touch with the plight of the French populace. Pamphleteers and caricaturists capitalized on this disconnect, creating vivid portrayals of Marie Antoinette as the epitome of excess and indulgence. One of the most notorious images depicted her as a glutton, feasting while her subjects starved, a potent symbol of the monarchy's disconnect from reality.

The press, still a relatively new and powerful medium, played a significant role in shaping public perception. The rise of pamphlet literature allowed dissenters to voice their grievances and spread anti-monarchical sentiment. These pamphlets often exaggerated the Queen's excesses, depicting her as a foreign interloper who had corrupted the French court. In a culture that thrived on gossip and scandal, Marie Antoinette became the subject of countless rumors. The infamous phrase "Let them eat cake," though never confirmed to have been uttered by her, epitomized how the public viewed her as ignorant of the struggles of the common people. This quote, which suggested a callous dismissal of their hunger, fed the growing resentment towards her and the monarchy.

The Queen's foreign origins further complicated her standing with the French people. As an Austrian archduchess, Marie Antoinette was seen by many as an outsider, a symbol of the Habsburg dynasty's perceived threat to French sovereignty. This perception was exacerbated by the political alliances and conflicts between France and Austria, particularly during the Seven Years' War and later tensions during the Revolutionary period. Her attempts to navigate the complex political landscape only served to alienate her further from her subjects. As the revolution gained momentum in the late 1780s, many viewed her not only as a foreigner but also as a key player in the monarchy's failures.

In 1785, the Diamond Necklace Affair served as a turning point in the public perception of Marie Antoinette. This scandal involved a fraudulent scheme to acquire a lavish diamond necklace worth an astronomical sum, which the Queen had no intention of purchasing. However, the scandal quickly spiraled out of control, with the Queen's name entangled in the web of deceit. The public was quick to judge, perceiving her as greedy and manipulative. The affair exacerbated existing resentments, and her reputation suffered immensely. The propaganda machine was relentless; pamphlets depicted her as a scheming seductress, further tarnishing her image and reinforcing negative perceptions.

Amidst the rising tide of anti-monarchical sentiment, Marie Antoinette's attempts to counteract the negative portrayals often fell flat. She engaged in various public relations efforts, including charitable endeavors and attempts to present herself as a devoted mother and compassionate queen. However, these efforts were often overshadowed by the relentless tide of negative press. The public remained unconvinced, and her words and actions were scrutinized through a lens of skepticism. The public's perception of her was solidified; she was seen as a lavish figurehead, incapable of understanding the struggles of her people.

The public's perception of Marie Antoinette was further complicated by the emergence of revolutionary rhetoric that painted the monarchy as a relic of a bygone era. The Enlightenment, with its emphasis on reason and equality, challenged the traditional structures of power, and the Queen became emblematic of the old regime. As revolutionary ideas took root, Marie Antoinette was increasingly portrayed as an obstacle to progress, a figure who epitomized the excesses of a decaying monarchy that needed to be dismantled. Her very existence became synonymous with the oppression and inequality that the revolution sought to overthrow.

As tensions escalated, the Queen found herself navigating a treacherous landscape marked by hostility and distrust. The political climate grew more volatile, and the public's perception morphed into a narrative of betrayal and excess. Marie Antoinette became less a person and more a symbol of everything that was wrong with the monarchy. Her fate became intertwined with the fate of the regime itself, and as the revolution gathered momentum, she was no longer simply the Queen; she was the embodiment of a system that many sought to dismantle.

The propaganda machine, which had once celebrated her beauty and charm, now turned against her with ferocity. Caricatures depicted her as a monstrous figure, her head adorned with crowns of bread, a stark reminder of the hunger that gripped the nation. As the revolutionaries rallied the populace, they used her image to galvanize support for their cause, portraying her as the epitome of royal excess that must be eradicated for the greater good. The narrative of Marie Antoinette as a villainous figure became entrenched, and her every move was scrutinized in light of this portrayal.

In the waning days of the monarchy, as the storming of the Bastille and subsequent revolts shook the very foundations of France, Marie Antoinette's public perception became a powerful weapon wielded by her enemies. The once-celebrated queen found herself trapped in a narrative crafted by her adversaries, her life a cautionary tale of the perils of power and the fragility of reputation. As the revolutionary fervor escalated, the Queen's identity as a figure of luxury and scandal solidified her tragic trajectory, culminating in a fate that would forever alter the course of history and the legacy of the French monarchy.

In the summer of 1785, Paris was abuzz with whispers of scandal and intrigue, a reflection of the growing discontent among its citizens. At the center of this tempest, an event unfolded that would come to symbolize the excesses of the French monarchy and exacerbate the tensions leading to revolution: the Diamond Necklace Affair. This scandal would not only tarnish the reputation of Marie Antoinette but also serve as a catalyst for the burgeoning resentment against the monarchy, positioning the queen as a focal point of public ire.

The Diamond Necklace Affair began with an extravagant jewel, a necklace of unparalleled brilliance and opulence crafted by the celebrated jeweler, Charles Böhmer. Commissioned originally for Madame de Pompadour, Louis XV's mistress, the necklace comprised an astounding 647 diamonds, totaling over 2,800 carats. After Pompadour's death, it remained unsold, becoming a symbol of unattainable luxury. The ambitious and unscrupulous Countess de La Motte would soon see it as an opportunity to exploit the vulnerabilities of the royal court.

The Countess de La Motte concocted a cunning scheme, leveraging her connections and a deep understanding of the court's dynamics. She forged letters and even fabricated a secret correspondence between herself and Marie Antoinette, purporting that the queen was interested in acquiring the necklace but lacked the immediate funds to do so. La Motte's audacity was matched only by her cunning; she convinced Cardinal de Rohan, a high-ranking clergyman and a man besotted with the queen, that he could win her favor by purchasing the necklace on her behalf.

Rohan, eager to win Antoinette's affection and perhaps to gain a semblance of influence at court, fell for the ruse. He was led to believe that he was involved in a clandestine affair with the queen, who would repay him in due time. As proof of her interest, La Motte produced what she claimed was a letter from Antoinette, sealed with a wax emblem that, unbeknownst to Rohan, was a mere forgery. The countess even arranged a meeting disguised as the queen, further deepening the deception.

Despite the inherent absurdity of the situation, Rohan proceeded to buy the necklace, believing he was fulfilling the queen's unspoken desire. The transaction, which amounted to an exorbitant sum of 1.6 million livres (a staggering fortune at the time), raised eyebrows among those who were aware. However, the court was so steeped in intrigue and personal ambition that many chose to turn a blind eye to the escalating scandal.

The necklace was never intended for Marie Antoinette. After the purchase, La Motte and her accomplices turned the jewels into cash, effectively stealing from the Cardinal and the crown alike. Their scheme unraveled when the Countess's extravagant lifestyle drew the attention of authorities. In 1786, as the truth began to surface, the scandal erupted into public consciousness with the force of a cannon blast.

As the details of the affair emerged, Marie Antoinette found herself unjustly ensnared in a web of deceit. The queen's reputation, which had already been marred by her extravagant lifestyle, suffered grievously at the hands of public perception. The accusation that she had orchestrated the entire scheme to acquire the necklace only added fuel to the fire. The press, increasingly hostile towards the monarchy, seized upon the scandal, portraying the queen as a figure of grotesque excess and moral decay. Pamphlets and caricatures circulated widely, depicting her as a spendthrift, a manipulator, and a harbinger of the monarchy's inevitable downfall.

The Diamond Necklace Affair not only damaged Marie Antoinette's reputation but also had profound political implications. It became a lightning rod for the frustrations of the populace, who were suffering from economic instability and food shortages. The lavishness of the court, embodied in the queen's ostentatious lifestyle, stood in stark contrast to the plight of ordinary citizens. As the public's anger grew, the monarchy's legitimacy came under siege.

In an effort to reclaim her tarnished image, Marie Antoinette sought to distance herself from the affair. During the trial of the Countess de La Motte in 1786, the queen's name was invoked repeatedly, yet she took no part in the proceedings. Instead, she remained sequestered in her private chambers, choosing to maintain a veneer of royal dignity amidst the chaos. However, her absence only seemed to amplify her perceived guilt in the eyes of the public.

The trials and tribulations of the Diamond Necklace Affair culminated in a public trial that showcased the disarray within the royal court. The Countess was found guilty of fraud, but the damage had already been done. The queen's association with the scandal would linger in the collective memory of the French populace, branding her as a figure of scandal and excess at a time when the winds of change were beginning to blow through France.

In the wake of the affair, Marie Antoinette attempted to rehabilitate her image by engaging in charitable works and trying to connect with the common people. Yet, the damage to her reputation was irreversible. The Diamond Necklace Affair stood as a testament to the frailty of royal power and the growing chasm between the monarchy and the people. It highlighted the precarious position of a queen perceived as out of touch with the struggles of her subjects, setting the stage for the tragic events that would follow in the years leading up to the revolution.

Ultimately, the scandal served as a harbinger of the revolution that was to come. It encapsulated the discontent simmering beneath the surface of French society, revealing the fragile nature of royal authority in an age of enlightenment and burgeoning democratic ideals. As Marie Antoinette's story unfolded, the specter of the Diamond Necklace Affair would haunt her, a relentless reminder of the price of excess and the volatility of public opinion.

Chapter 7: Family and Personal Struggles

The transition into motherhood marked a significant turning point in Marie Antoinette's life, a moment where her identity began to evolve from the frivolous young queen to a figure of maternal responsibility. At the age of 19, she gave birth to her first child, a daughter named Marie-Thérèse, on December 19, 1778. This event was met with great fanfare, not merely because of the joy it brought to the royal couple but due to the broader implications for the French monarchy. The birth of an heir was crucial in securing the future of the Bourbon lineage and calming the political anxieties that loomed over the nation.

Marie Antoinette's experience as a new mother was defined by both joy and apprehension. The expectations placed upon her were immense; she was acutely aware that the survival of the monarchy hinged on her ability to produce a male heir. This societal pressure weighed heavily on her shoulders, adding layers of complexity to her role as queen. Despite the lavish celebrations surrounding her daughter's birth, the question of when a son would arrive lingered in the air like an unspoken challenge.

In the early days of motherhood, Marie Antoinette found solace in the bonds she formed with her children. She was known to have a genuine affection for her daughter, taking great delight in her milestones and cherishing the moments they shared. The queen would often engage in playful interactions with Marie-Thérèse, dressing her in the latest fashions and allowing her to accompany her in the opulent halls of Versailles. Yet, the reality of royal motherhood came with restrictions; the queen was constantly reminded of her public duties and the need to maintain an image of regal composure.

As time went on, Marie Antoinette's anxieties grew as the birth of a male heir remained elusive. The pressure intensified with each passing year. After Marie-Thérèse, she gave birth to a second daughter, Sophie, in 1786, followed by another girl, Louise, in 1787. Each birth was celebrated, yet the absence of a son left many at court whispering doubts about the queen's capacity to fulfill her most important duty. The pressure from her mother, Empress Maria Theresa of Austria, also loomed large. The empress had written her daughter letters filled with maternal advice, emphasizing the importance of producing a male heir and the expectations that came with her role. These letters, though filled with love, served as constant reminders of Marie Antoinette's perceived failures.

The queen's marital relationship with Louis XVI also came under scrutiny during these years. Although they had formed a deep bond, the couple struggled to consummate their marriage for several years, which added to the pressure on Marie Antoinette. Their union was often described in the court as lacking passion, leading to speculation that the king was disinterested in fulfilling his royal duties. This perception not only affected their personal lives but also fueled the public's growing disdain for the monarchy. Observers scrutinized every aspect of the royal couple's life, and when Marie Antoinette did not bear a son, many placed the blame squarely on her shoulders.

The situation became more dire when, in 1781, Marie Antoinette finally gave birth to a son, Louis-Joseph, duc de Normandie. The birth was celebrated with grand festivities throughout France, as the nation rejoiced in securing the future of the Bourbon dynasty. For Marie Antoinette, this moment was bittersweet; while she felt a sense of relief and accomplishment, the constant scrutiny and expectations remained. The joy of motherhood was often shadowed by the reality that her children were not merely her offspring but were seen as political pawns in the game of royal alliances.

The queen's dedication to her children was apparent in the ways she attempted to create a nurturing environment within the confines of the palace. Despite the rigid protocols of court life, she sought to cultivate a sense of normalcy for her children. Marie Antoinette personally oversaw their education, emphasizing the importance of instilling virtues of kindness, humility, and loyalty. She hired tutors who were tasked not only with teaching them the arts and sciences but also with shaping their characters. The queen would often play the role of a doting mother, taking her children on walks through the gardens of Versailles or hosting small family gatherings, allowing her to escape the harsh realities of court politics, if only for a moment.

However, the queen's maternal instincts were often at odds with her public persona. As the financial crisis in France deepened, the image of the lavish lifestyle of the royal family became increasingly out of touch with the struggles of the common people. Marie Antoinette's attempts to foster a maternal image were complicated by her status as a foreign queen, often viewed with suspicion and resentment. The public's perception of her as a lavish spender only intensified, and the birth of her heir could not quell the tide of discontent that was sweeping across France.

In 1789, as the revolution began to take shape, the queen's relationship with her children became even more strained. The monarchy faced unprecedented turmoil, and the once-celebrated royal family was now being scrutinized for every move they made. The queen's protective instincts kicked in as she attempted to shield her children from the growing unrest, but her efforts were increasingly futile as the revolution escalated. The fear of losing her children became a haunting reality, especially as the monarchy's grip on power weakened.

Marie Antoinette's journey through motherhood was marked by deep love and profound challenges. It was a testament to her resilience as she navigated the complexities of royal life under the weight of expectations and societal pressures. As she endeavored to be a loving mother while fulfilling her role as queen, she would ultimately become a symbol of both the opulence and the fragility of the monarchy. The legacy of her motherhood would echo through the annals of history, intertwining with her tragic fate and the fortunes of France itself.

Marie Antoinette's life was not merely a tapestry woven with threads of luxury and privilege; it was also marked by deep personal losses that carved shadows across her heart. These losses were not merely the result of court intrigues or the tumult of political upheaval; they were intimate, profound, and deeply felt, shaping her into the woman she would ultimately become.

In the early years of her marriage to Louis XVI, Marie Antoinette's joy was overshadowed by the pressure to produce an heir. For a young queen, the birth of a child was more than an act of motherhood; it was a matter of state, an assurance of the monarchy's continuity. The couple's first child, Marie-Thérèse, was born on December 19, 1778, and for a time, this event brought a sense of fulfillment and relief. However, the subsequent births of two children—Louis Joseph and Louis Charles—were marked by tragedy. Louis Joseph died at a tender age of seven in 1787, succumbing to tuberculosis. This loss reverberated through the royal household, a stark reminder of the fragility of life and the responsibilities that weighed upon her. Marie Antoinette's grief was palpable; she had lost not just a child but a piece of her own heart.

In the aftermath of Louis Joseph's death, Marie Antoinette found herself grappling with a profound sense of emptiness. As a mother, she had invested her hopes and dreams in her children, and the death of her son shattered the illusion of control she once held over her life. In the opulent halls of Versailles, she was surrounded by luxury, yet the loss of her child cast a pall over her existence. The queen, who had once been the epitome of joy and vitality, became a figure of quiet sorrow, often retreating into her private quarters to mourn away from the prying eyes of the court.

As if fate had not dealt her enough sorrow, Marie Antoinette's personal tragedies continued with the death of her mother, Maria Theresa, in 1780.

The Empress of Austria had been a guiding force in her life, a symbol of strength and wisdom. Her mother's death was a seismic event that left Marie Antoinette feeling adrift in a world that had suddenly become more complex and unforgiving. The empress had been a source of counsel and support, and her absence left a void that could not easily be filled. The queen was now a mother and a wife, but at times she felt like a child, lost without her mother's guidance to navigate the treacherous waters of court politics and familial expectations.

In her grief, Marie Antoinette sought solace in her children, especially her remaining son, Louis Charles. She lavished affection upon him, determined to shield him from the sorrows that had befallen her. Yet, the specter of loss loomed large, and she was painfully aware of the precariousness of life in the royal family. The specter of disease and death was ever-present, and she could only hope that her remaining children would be spared the fates that had befallen their siblings.

These personal losses were compounded by the strains of her royal duties. The pressures of court life did little to alleviate her grief; instead, they often exacerbated her sense of isolation. The court of Versailles, with its elaborate rituals and endless intrigues, felt increasingly suffocating. The very same courtiers who had once fawned over her were now whispering behind her back, their eyes filled with judgment and scorn. The queen's extravagant lifestyle, once a source of delight, became a target for criticism, particularly after the untimely deaths of her children. It was as if she had become a lightning rod for the discontent of the populace, and her personal tragedies were twisted into narratives of failure and excess.

In the face of such relentless scrutiny, Marie Antoinette sought refuge in her closest companions. She cultivated relationships with a select few who provided comfort, laughter, and distraction from the harsh realities of her life. Yet, even these friendships were fraught with tension, as the court was rife with rivalries and jealousies. The queen's affections were often exploited by those who sought to gain favor or advance their own agendas. Betrayal became a frequent companion, further deepening her sense of solitude.

Compounding her grief was the recognition that her position as queen rendered her vulnerable to the whims of fortune. The very privileges that defined her existence also served to isolate her from the world outside the gilded gates of Versailles. The queen could not afford to grieve openly; her role demanded strength and composure, even as her heart ached with the weight of sorrow. It was a delicate balance, one that many in her position struggled to maintain, but for Marie Antoinette, it felt particularly burdensome.

As the years wore on, her losses began to transform her. The woman who had once reveled in the splendor of her surroundings found herself drawn to quieter pastimes. The Petit Trianon, with its more intimate setting, became a sanctuary where she could engage in simple pleasures—gardening, music, and the company of a few trusted friends. Here, she could momentarily escape the pressures of court life and indulge in the joys of motherhood, albeit tinged with the memories of her lost children.

Yet, the joys of the present were often overshadowed by the grief of the past. Marie Antoinette became adept at masking her emotions, projecting an image of strength even as she felt herself unraveling inside. The façade of the queen was one of elegance and composure, but behind closed doors, she wrestled with the demons of despair. The deaths of her children and her mother were not merely personal losses; they were profound reminders of the fragility of life and the burdens of her royal status.

In these moments of respite, Marie Antoinette often contemplated her legacy. Would she be remembered as a queen who indulged in extravagance, or as a mother who faced unimaginable losses with resilience? Despite the tumult that surrounded her, she remained steadfast in her desire to find meaning in her life, to transform her grief into a source of strength. It was a struggle that would accompany her throughout her life, shaping her character and informing her decisions as the tides of revolution began to rise around her.

In many ways, the losses Marie Antoinette endured were a prelude to the greater tragedies that awaited her in the years to come. Yet, within the depths of her sorrow lay a flicker of resilience—a determination to navigate the complexities of her existence with grace, even as the world around her began to shift in ways she could scarcely comprehend.

In the years leading up to the French Revolution, Marie Antoinette found herself navigating a treacherous landscape of political unrest and personal turmoil. Her marriage to Louis XVI had initially appeared to be a union of hope and promise, but as the country spiraled into financial crisis and social discord, the weight of the crown grew heavier on her shoulders. The Queen, once a symbol of opulence and grace, became acutely aware of her precarious position in a court that was increasingly hostile to her presence.

Amid the growing discontent, Marie Antoinette attempted to assert her influence over the monarchy's direction, motivated by a desire to protect her family and maintain stability within the realm. She recognized that

France was not merely struggling with economic woes but was also grappling with a profound existential crisis. The enlightenment ideas that had begun to permeate the courts and salons were fostering a sense of entitlement among the populace, who were growing weary of the extravagance displayed by the royal family while they faced dire hardship. In this tumultuous atmosphere, Marie Antoinette sought avenues for reform that could potentially alleviate the suffering of her subjects and restore her waning popularity.

The Queen's first significant initiative aimed at reform was her involvement in the promotion of agricultural improvements. Understanding that a nation's strength lies in its ability to feed its people, she championed projects that focused on enhancing agricultural productivity. Inspired by her upbringing in the Habsburg court, where she had witnessed the importance of self-sufficiency, Marie Antoinette supported the establishment of model farms and agricultural fairs. She believed that by showcasing successful farming techniques, she could inspire the nobility and commoners alike to invest in the land, thereby fostering a sense of national pride and unity.

However, her attempts to address the agricultural crisis were met with considerable skepticism. Many viewed her efforts as superficial, dismissing her as out of touch with the realities faced by the average French citizen. As rumors circulated regarding her extravagant spending on fashion and luxury, her credibility faltered, and the populace's resentment deepened. The irony was not lost on the Queen: as she endeavored to promote reform, the very image of her life seemed to contradict her intentions. The gap between her lavish lifestyle and the struggles of her subjects became a focal point for critics, who used it to fuel the flames of revolution.

Marie Antoinette also sought to influence her husband, Louis XVI, to adopt more progressive policies. The King, who was often indecisive and reluctant to take bold action, found himself swayed by the pressures of his advisors, many of whom were hesitant to embrace change. The Queen's efforts to persuade him to support financial reforms, including the taxation of the privileged classes, faced insurmountable resistance from the nobility, who were unwilling to relinquish their tax exemptions. This entrenched opposition only solidified Marie Antoinette's reputation as the foreigner whose presence threatened the very foundation of the French monarchy.

Despite the challenges, Marie Antoinette was not deterred. In a remarkable display of resilience, she turned her attention to the welfare of the impoverished. She established charitable organizations and initiatives aimed at providing aid to the needy, particularly during times of famine. The Queen's compassion resonated with some, and her efforts to alleviate suffering earned her a modicum of respect among the more progressive factions of society. However, these positive gestures frequently went unnoticed, overshadowed by the prevailing narrative that painted her as a callous figure indifferent to the plight of her people.

In the late 1780s, as political tensions escalated, Marie Antoinette's attempts at reform became increasingly desperate. She perceived the rising tide of revolutionary fervor as an existential threat to her family and the monarchy. In her mind, the survival of her children and the preservation of the royal legacy depended on her willingness to resist the encroaching change. She advocated for a return to traditional values and sought to rally support from the nobility and the clergy, urging them to stand united against the revolutionary forces that threatened to dismantle their way of life.

Yet, her resistance was met with a growing tide of opposition. The populace, emboldened by the rhetoric of liberty and equality, began to view the royal family as out of touch with the reality of their lives. The Queen's attempts to hold on to the status quo were seen as obstacles to progress, and her efforts to rally support were increasingly met with derision. The more she clung to the idea of royal privilege, the more alienated she became from her subjects. The revolutionaries painted her as the embodiment of the monarchy's excesses, and the public spectacle of her life became a potent symbol of everything that was wrong with France.

In the midst of this turmoil, Marie Antoinette's personal struggles deepened. The pressures of court life and the relentless scrutiny of her actions took a toll on her mental and emotional well-being. As her family's fortunes waned, she grappled with feelings of helplessness and despair. The Queen's once-vibrant spirit began to dim, overshadowed by the weight of her responsibilities and the fear of losing everything she held dear.

As the Revolution gathered momentum, Marie Antoinette found herself at a crossroads. Her attempts at reform and resistance became increasingly futile, and she began to realize that the world she had known was slipping away. The very ideals she had fought to uphold were now being wielded against her, transforming her from a celebrated queen into a figure of scorn and vilification. While her heart longed for a return to the glory of the past, the reality of her situation demanded a reckoning with the present—a stark reminder that the tides of history were shifting, and her place in it was far from secure.

Caught in a web of ambition, loyalty, and tragedy, Marie Antoinette stood at the precipice of a new era, one that would forever alter the course of French history and redefine her legacy. The attempts she made at reform were not merely political maneuvers; they were desperate bids for redemption in a world that had turned against her. As the Revolution unfolded, she would learn the hard truth that sometimes, even the most well-meaning efforts can become entangled in the complexities of power and perception. In her quest to protect her family and forge a path toward reconciliation, Marie Antoinette's journey would culminate in a confrontation with destiny that would echo through the annals of history.

Chapter 8: The Revolution Begins: Fall from Grace

The summer of 1789 heralded a seismic shift in the fabric of French society, as resentment and discontent coalesced into a fervent demand for change. The streets of Paris, once resplendent with the opulence of the monarchy, were now charged with a palpable tension, a powder keg waiting for a spark. On July 14, 1789, that spark ignited, and the storming of the Bastille became a defining moment not only for the revolution but also for Marie Antoinette, who stood at the center of this tumultuous period, her life forever altered by the unfolding chaos.

The Bastille, a fortress prison that loomed ominously over the eastern edge of Paris, was a symbol of royal authority and oppression. Its very existence represented the old regime, and for the people, it embodied the tyranny of the monarchy. For many Parisians, it was not merely a prison; it was a bastion of injustice, where dissenters were silenced, and the king's will was enforced with brutal efficiency. As rumors spread that King Louis XVI was amassing troops around Paris to quash the growing unrest, the tension escalated. The cries for liberty and justice resonated through the city, uniting disparate factions of society in a common cause.

Marie Antoinette, isolated in her gilded cage at Versailles, was acutely aware of the discontent brewing among her subjects. In her mind, the queen still clung to the hope that her lavish lifestyle and the pomp of the court could distract from the economic hardships faced by ordinary citizens. Yet, as the days rolled into weeks, the whispers of rebellion grew louder, and the reality of her situation became inescapable. Like many of her contemporaries, she underestimated the depth of the people's anger, believing that their loyalty to the crown would prevail. Yet, as the cries for change echoed through the streets, the foundations of her world began to crumble.

On the morning of July 14, the atmosphere in Paris was electric. The sun rose over a city brimming with anticipation and uncertainty. Groups of citizens, fueled by a mix of fear and determination, mobilized, armed with makeshift weapons – pikes, clubs, and whatever they could muster. They were not just angry; they were desperate, driven by hunger and a yearning for dignity. As news spread that the Bastille had been a repository of gunpowder, the prisoners within its walls took on a new significance. The storming of the fortress was no longer just a matter of freeing the incarcerated; it was a mission to seize arms and assert their rights against a tyrannical regime.

The tension culminated in the early afternoon when a throng of revolutionaries, numbering in the thousands, converged on the Bastille. As they approached the fortress, cries of "Liberty!" rang out, echoing against the stone walls. The governor of the Bastille, Bernard-René de Launay, was in an increasingly precarious position. Faced with an overwhelming crowd, he ordered his men to prepare for a defense. What began as a standoff quickly escalated into violence as shots rang out, igniting the fury of the besiegers. In the chaos that ensued, the Bastille's gates were breached, and the revolutionaries surged into the fortress, determined to claim their victory.

Inside, the atmosphere was frantic. The defenders, outnumbered and outmatched, fought valiantly but ultimately succumbed to the tide of anger and desperation. As the dust settled, the revolutionaries emerged victorious, parading the severed heads of the governor and his men on pikes through the streets of Paris. The fall of the Bastille sent shockwaves throughout the city, igniting a revolutionary fervor that would soon engulf the entire nation. The cries of "Liberty, Equality, Fraternity" became the rallying cry of the burgeoning movement, a stark contrast to the values that Marie Antoinette had long upheld.

News of the Bastille's fall reached Versailles, and the royal court was thrown into a state of panic. The once-imposing walls of the palace, which had sheltered the queen from the outside world, now felt like a fragile façade. Marie Antoinette, who had spent years entangled in the web of court intrigue and luxury, found herself facing a reality that was increasingly threatening. The whispers of revolution were no longer distant; they were at her doorstep, and the specter of her past missteps loomed large. The lavish parties and extravagant gowns that had defined her reign now seemed grotesque against the backdrop of a nation in turmoil.

In the days that followed, the queen's advisors urged her to remain calm and reassured her that the loyalty of the military would protect them. Yet, the queen found it increasingly difficult to stave off her fears. As she sat in her private chambers, surrounded by opulence, she could hear the distant echoes of revolution reverberating through the halls of Versailles. The palace, once a sanctuary of luxury, felt suffocating, and the laughter that had once filled its corridors now seemed a haunting reminder of her disconnectedness from the plight of her people.

The storming of the Bastille marked more than just the physical confrontation between the monarchy and the revolutionaries; it was a turning point in the perception of Marie Antoinette herself. The queen, who had once been viewed as a foreign interloper, now became a symbol of excess and disconnect. The people's grievances transformed her from a figure of fascination to one of contempt. As pamphlets and caricatures depicting her as a lavish spendthrift circulated through the streets, the queen's image was tarnished, and her ability to govern in the hearts of her subjects diminished.

Amidst the upheaval, Marie Antoinette found herself grappling with her identity. She had been raised to be a queen, to embody the ideals of her station, yet she was now confronted with a reality where those ideals were being dismantled. The fall of the Bastille was not merely an event; it was a harbinger of the profound changes that awaited her and the monarchy. As the revolution unfolded its consequences, Marie Antoinette's life of luxury would soon yield to a narrative of scandal and tragedy, forever altering her legacy and the course of French history.

The air in the Tuileries Palace was thick with an oppressive silence, an unsettling contrast to the vibrant life that had once pulsed through the halls of Versailles. Once the proud residence of the French monarchy, the Tuileries had become a gilded cage for Marie Antoinette and her family. The echoes of laughter, music, and grand festivities that had characterized her early years as queen were replaced by whispers of dissent and the heavy footfalls of guards. The opulence of her surroundings, once a source of comfort and security, now served as a grim reminder of her fall from grace.

In the early days of their captivity, the royal family clung to the hope that the turmoil erupting outside would soon pass, that the voices of the revolutionaries would fade into the background, allowing them to reclaim their lives. Marie Antoinette often gazed out of the palace windows, her heart heavy with longing for the lush gardens of the Petit Trianon, where she had found solace in nature's embrace. Now, the gardens lay beyond her reach, a symbol of freedom lost. The once-flourishing realm of her dreams had transformed into a battleground of ideology, where her very existence was called into question.

As the days turned into weeks, the queen's role shifted from that of a revered monarch to a figure of public scrutiny and derision. The revolutionary fervor that had swept through France painted her not as a beloved queen but as a symbol of excess and privilege, a target in the crosshairs of an enraged populace. The press, once a tool for royal propaganda, turned against her, distorting her image and amplifying the grievances of the people. The infamous pamphlets and caricatures that circulated through Paris depicted her as a decadent foreigner, a woman consumed by extravagance while her subjects suffered from hunger and despair. This relentless attack on her character seeped into the minds of the citizens, further isolating her from the very people she had once been meant to serve.

In the Tuileries, the atmosphere was charged with anxiety and uncertainty. Marie Antoinette struggled to maintain a façade of dignity while her heart raced with fear for her children and her husband, King Louis XVI. The revolutionary government had stripped the monarchy of its power, and the royal family was now dependent on the goodwill of their captors. The queen sought to shield her children from the growing tensions, attempting to create a sense of normalcy amidst the chaos. She organized games and storytime, drawing on her own memories of childhood to provide comfort and distraction. Yet, the laughter of her children felt hollow, like a fragile bubble that could burst at any moment.

As the months dragged on, the queen's isolation deepened. The once-bustling court that had surrounded her was now reduced to a small circle of loyalists and guards. Many former courtiers had either fled or joined the revolutionary cause, and those who remained were often driven by fear rather than loyalty. Marie Antoinette found solace in the companionship of her closest confidantes, including the steadfast Madame de Campan, who offered both practical advice and emotional support. Together, they navigated the treacherous waters of court politics, seeking to maintain a semblance of order in their disrupted lives.

Yet, the queen's efforts were often thwarted by the reality of her situation. The National Assembly, increasingly emboldened, sought to consolidate its power by dismantling the institutions that had upheld the monarchy. In June 1791, the royal family's ill-fated attempt to escape Paris, known as the Flight to Varennes, would prove to be a turning point in their captivity. The plan, crafted in secret and fueled by desperation, was a perilous gamble that aimed to reunite the royal family with loyal supporters in the countryside. However, their flight was thwarted when they were recognized in Varennes and forcibly returned to Paris, further humiliating the monarchy and solidifying the perception of the royals as prisoners in their own land.

Following the failed escape, the atmosphere within the Tuileries became increasingly tense. The queen found herself surrounded by guards who were once her subjects, now transformed into watchful eyes that scrutinized her every move. The walls that had once echoed with the sounds of joyous celebrations now bore witness to her growing despair. The queen's dreams of returning to a life of luxury and power seemed impossibly distant, replaced by the grim reality of her circumstances.

In the midst of this turmoil, Marie Antoinette's resilience began to emerge. She understood that her survival depended on her ability to adapt, to navigate the complex web of revolutionary politics with grace and cunning. The queen sought to engage with the changing political landscape, attempting to win the favor of influential figures within the revolutionary government. She wrote letters, appealing to their sense of humanity and urging them to spare her family from the growing tide of hatred. In these letters, she portrayed herself as a mother, a woman who shared the same concerns and fears as the citizenry, hoping to evoke empathy in those who held her fate in their hands.

Despite her attempts to connect with the revolutionaries, the gulf between the monarchy and the people widened. The storming of the Tuileries on August 10, 1792, marked a critical juncture in her captivity. The palace was besieged by an angry mob, determined to overthrow the monarchy once and for all. The queen and her family were forced into hiding within the palace, their safety hanging by a thread. The specter of violence loomed ever closer, and the walls that had once stood as a testament to royal power now felt like a prison closing in around her.

As she faced the reality of her dwindling power, Marie Antoinette's spirit remained unbroken, a testament to her strength as a woman and a mother. She clung to her family, fiercely protective of her children amid the chaos. In those moments of despair, she drew strength from the bond they shared, reminding herself that even in captivity, she was still a queen and a mother. The once-splendid life she had known was gone, but her resolve to protect her children, to safeguard their future, remained steadfast.

The Tuileries Palace had become a microcosm of the turmoil enveloping France, a place where the dreams of a queen collided with the harsh realities of revolution. Marie Antoinette's captivity was not merely a physical imprisonment; it was a crucible that would test her resilience, her identity, and ultimately, her legacy. The world outside may have turned against her, but within the confines of her heart, the spirit of a queen endured, a flickering flame amidst the gathering darkness.

As the revolutionary fervor engulfed France, the atmosphere within the Tuileries Palace grew increasingly oppressive. The echoes of discontent resonated not just through the streets of Paris but also within the very walls that had once reverberated with laughter and celebration. Marie Antoinette, once the epitome of luxury and grace, now found herself ensnared in a web of political turmoil and personal despair. The Queen's situation was dire; the royal family's safety was threatened, and the only way to escape the tightening noose of revolution was to flee.

The idea of flight was fraught with peril, yet it was one that had taken root in Marie Antoinette's mind. The Queen was acutely aware that her position was increasingly untenable. The mob that had stormed the Bastille in July 1789 was merely the harbinger of a much larger storm. The common people, once enamored with her beauty and fashion, were now growing disillusioned with the monarchy's extravagance amidst their suffering. In this climate of hostility, the royal family found themselves more prisoners than sovereigns.

In the spring of 1791, the tension became unbearable. Marie Antoinette and her husband, King Louis XVI, began to seriously contemplate a flight to safety. They envisioned a retreat to the eastern frontier of France, where loyalist sympathies still lingered. It was a desperate gambit, but one that offered a glimmer of hope for a restoration of royal authority. The Queen's brother, Leopold II of Austria, had encouraged the move, suggesting that if the royal family could reach a safe haven, they could rally support from foreign powers to restore the monarchy.

The planning was clandestine, shrouded in secrecy, for the slightest whisper could lead to their undoing. The Queen turned to her trusted confidant, Count Axel von Fersen, a Swedish nobleman who had long harbored feelings for her. Fersen, with his connections and knowledge of the political landscape, became the linchpin of the escape plan. Together, they devised a route that would take the royal family through the countryside, avoiding the watchful eyes of revolutionary sympathizers.

As the days passed, the tension mounted. Marie Antoinette was acutely aware of the stakes; failure would mean not only her own demise but also that of her children and her husband. The Queen's heart raced with a mix of fear and exhilaration as the night of June 20, 1791, approached. Disguised in plain clothing, the royal family would leave the Tuileries Palace under the cover of darkness, concealed within a carriage.

The evening arrived, cloaked in a shroud of anxiety. The royal family gathered in the palace, their hearts heavy with the weight of uncertainty. Louis XVI, typically seen as the indecisive monarch, seemed resolute as they prepared for their escape. Marie Antoinette, despite her regal upbringing, was transformed into a mother willing to do anything to protect her children, even if it meant stepping into the shadows. She took one last look at the opulent rooms that had once been her prison and steeled herself for the journey ahead.

As they slipped into the night, the streets of Paris lay quiet, but an undercurrent of tension vibrated in the air. Unknown to them, their departure had already been discovered. Loyalists within the Tuileries had caught wind of the escape and alerted the revolutionary factions. The royal family, oblivious to the brewing storm, continued their journey, their hearts pounding in unison with the rhythmic clatter of the carriage wheels.

The initial leg of their escape took them towards the eastern provinces, with the intention of reaching the town of Varennes. But as dawn broke and the first rays of light illuminated the countryside, they encountered a series of obstacles that would prove insurmountable. They had not traveled far before they were halted by a checkpoint manned by revolutionaries. The tension escalated as the guards scrutinized the carriage, their suspicions growing with each passing moment.

In a fateful twist, one of the guards recognized the King, and a wave of panic swept through the royal family. The carriage was forced to stop, and the guards began to pull back the curtains. It was a desperate moment; the Queen's heart sank as they were unmasked. The illusion of anonymity shattered, and the reality of their situation came crashing down. The royal family was captured and taken back to Paris, their dreams of escape snuffed out.

The return to the Tuileries was a bitter humiliation. Marie Antoinette, once celebrated as the Queen of France, was now a symbol of the monarchy's failures. The public's mood shifted dramatically from adoration to scorn. The flight had not only failed but had also intensified the resentment that had been brewing against them. The Queen, who had once dazzled the court with her charm and poise, now faced the caustic glare of a populace that had turned its back on her.

In the days that followed, Marie Antoinette's fate grew increasingly precarious. The revolutionary government, seeking to solidify its power, used the failed escape attempt as a rallying cry against the monarchy. The Queen became a focal point of anger, a representation of everything the revolution sought to dismantle. The whispers of her extravagance and the perceived conspiracies surrounding her began to circulate with renewed vigor.

The failed flight to Varennes marked a pivotal moment in Marie Antoinette's life. It was not merely a physical return to captivity but a symbolic descent into a darkness from which there would be no escape. The glimmer of hope that had accompanied her escape plan was extinguished, replaced by the harsh realities of impending doom. In the months that followed, the revolutionary tide would continue to swell, leading inexorably towards the cataclysmic events that would seal her fate.

The Queen, once a figure of luxury and elegance, was transformed into a tragic embodiment of a crumbling monarchy. The attempt to flee had illuminated the depths of her despair and the fragility of her existence, marking the beginning of the end for Marie Antoinette, the woman and the Queen.

Chapter 9: The Imprisoned Queen: Trials and Tribulations

As the sun rose over the Tuileries Palace, the oppressive atmosphere of confinement hung heavily in the air, a stark contrast to the grandeur that once defined Marie Antoinette's existence. The echoes of laughter and music that once filled the opulent halls were replaced by the whispers of discontent that permeated the hearts of the French people. The queen, who had once danced amidst the splendor of Versailles, now faced an unsettling reality: her royal privileges were slipping away like sand through her fingers.

The loss of royal privileges was not merely a matter of material wealth; it represented a profound shift in identity for a woman who had been raised to believe in the divine right of kings and queens. The Tuileries, which had once served as a royal residence and a symbol of power, had transformed into a gilded prison. The opulence of her past life, where every whim was catered to by servants, was now replaced with the stark limitations of imprisonment. Marie Antoinette found herself grappling not only with the loss of her status but also with the emotional toll it exacted on her spirit.

In the early days of her imprisonment, Marie Antoinette clung to the hope that her royal lineage would afford her some semblance of protection. She believed that the people would rally around her, recognizing her as a symbol of France's grandeur and stability. However, with each passing day, it became increasingly clear that the revolutionary fervor sweeping through the nation had obliterated any vestige of loyalty or affection that might have existed for the queen. Once celebrated for her beauty and style, she was now vilified as a symbol of excess and decadence. The disconnect between her past privileges and her present reality was stark, and the queen's sense of self began to unravel.

As the months dragged on, the queen was subjected to a series of humiliating restrictions that stripped her of the rights she had taken for granted. Gone were the days when she could summon her ladies-in-waiting at a moment's notice, or indulge in the luxuries of fine clothing and extravagant banquets. The once-bustling court, where she had wielded influence and charm, was now reduced to a handful of loyal attendants, who could do little to alleviate her growing despair. The isolation was suffocating, and the former queen could not escape the bitter irony of her situation: the very privileges that had once defined her were now the chains that bound her.

At the same time, the loss of royal privileges served as a harsh reminder of the shifting political landscape. The revolutionary government, intent on dismantling the remnants of the monarchy, was relentless in its efforts to undermine the authority of the queen. They prohibited her from communicating freely with her family and allies, further isolating her from the support she so desperately needed. Her once-cherished role as a mother was now marred by the pain of separation from her children, who had been taken from her in an effort to sever the last ties to her royal status. The emotional toll of these restrictions was immense, as Marie Antoinette grappled with feelings of helplessness and despair.

In an effort to retain a sense of agency, Marie Antoinette sought to adapt to her new environment. She filled her days with simple routines, attempting to find solace in the mundane. Often, she would take long walks within the confines of the Tuileries gardens, seeking comfort in the beauty of nature that had once surrounded her in the lavish gardens of Versailles. Yet, even this small pleasure was tinged with sadness, as the vibrant blooms reminded her of the life she had lost—a life filled with laughter, joy, and the unbridled freedom of a queen.

Her desire to maintain some semblance of dignity in the face of adversity led her to forge connections with the few individuals permitted to see her. She developed a rapport with her remaining attendants, who provided her with companionship during her darkest hours. These relationships, however fraught with the tension of their precarious circumstances, served as a lifeline for Marie Antoinette, reminding her that she was not entirely alone in her suffering. Yet, the reality of her situation was ever-present; she was a queen without a kingdom, a figure once revered who had become the subject of scorn and ridicule.

Despite these challenges, Marie Antoinette's spirit was not entirely crushed. She found herself reflecting on her past, drawing strength from memories of her earlier life. The lavish banquets, the laughter of her children, and the vibrant social gatherings at Versailles played out in her mind like a poignant film, offering a bittersweet escape from her current predicament. Yet, as these memories faded into the background of her imprisonment, they became a stark reminder of what she could never regain.

The loss of her privileges extended beyond the confines of the Tuileries. The queen became acutely aware of the changing public perception of her. Once celebrated as a trendsetter and a fashion icon, she was now viewed as a caricature of excess, vilified in pamphlets and broadsides that depicted her as an out-of-touch aristocrat. The very qualities that had once garnered admiration were twisted into weapons of propaganda, fueling public outrage against the monarchy. The queen's image, once carefully curated and celebrated, became a target for public derision, compounding her feelings of isolation.

As the revolutionary tide continued to swell, the loss of royal privileges marked a significant turning point in Marie Antoinette's life. It was not just the physical constraints of her imprisonment that weighed heavily upon her; it was the shattering of her identity as a queen and a mother, the erosion of her influence, and the relentless march of a new world order that rendered her a relic of a bygone era. The stark reality of her situation was a painful reminder that the privileges she had once wielded with grace had become the very chains that bound her, leading her inexorably toward a future of uncertainty, loss, and ultimately, tragedy.

The atmosphere within the Tuileries Palace was thick with tension and uncertainty as Marie Antoinette faced the harrowing reality of separation from her family. The revolution had turned her world upside down, and the regal life she once knew had become a distant memory. Once surrounded by the laughter of her children and the grandeur of the court, she now found herself in a prison of her own making, where walls seemed to echo the cries of the restless populace outside.

Marie Antoinette had always been a devoted mother, nurturing her children with affection and care. The bond she shared with her daughter, Marie-Thérèse, and her two sons, Louis-Charles and Louis-Joseph, was a source of solace amid the turmoil of court life. However, as the revolution escalated, the protective cocoon of familial love began to fray. The monarchy was under siege, and the safety of her children became a pressing concern. With each passing day, the distance between them grew, both physically and emotionally.

When the royal family was first escorted to the Tuileries in June 1789, they were met with a mix of skepticism and hostility from the people of Paris. The once-resplendent palace now served as a gilded cage, its opulence overshadowed by the threat of violence lurking beyond its walls. Marie Antoinette's maternal instincts kicked in as she sought to shield her children from the chaos swirling around them. She would often gather them close, telling them stories of their ancestors, instilling in them a sense of pride in their heritage while desperately trying to maintain some semblance of normalcy.

Yet, the reality of their predicament was inescapable. The royal family was watched closely, their movements monitored by an increasingly hostile populace. Rations dwindled, and the threat of hunger loomed over them. The children, once accustomed to the comforts of Versailles, now faced the stark contrast of their new existence. Marie Antoinette worked tirelessly to provide for her children, using what little resources she had to ensure their well-being. She created makeshift games and activities, attempting to distract them from the grim atmosphere that enveloped their home. Her heart ached as she witnessed the innocent joy of her children being overshadowed by the ever-present fear of what the future might hold.

As the revolutionary fervor intensified, the queen was torn between her duty to her family and her loyalty to her husband, King Louis XVI. Both parents felt the weight of their responsibilities, but as events unfolded, it became increasingly clear that their roles as monarchs were in direct conflict with their roles as parents. The family was isolated from the outside world, and communication with their extended family—both in France and Austria—became a fraught endeavor. The queen longed for news from her beloved mother, Maria Theresa, whose wise counsel had always guided her throughout her life. But the distance felt insurmountable, and letters went unanswered.

The situation became even more dire after the failed attempt to escape to Varennes in June 1791. The family's flight was intended to secure their safety; however, it ended in disaster, leading to their capture and subsequent return to Paris. Following this incident, the queen was separated from her children for the first time, her heart breaking as they were taken from her. In the eyes of the revolutionaries, the royal family represented everything that was wrong with France, and their children were seen as pawns in a greater political game.

As the months passed, the children were kept under close surveillance, further deepening Marie Antoinette's anguish. The queen was allowed occasional visits, but these moments were tinged with sorrow. She would sit across from her children, struggling to mask her despair as they clung to her, seeking comfort and reassurance. The sight of their innocent faces filled her with both love and heartbreak. They were so young, yet already burdened with the weight of their family's downfall. During these visits, she would try to impart wisdom and strength, telling them tales of resilience, but deep down, she feared for their futures.

The separation extended beyond physical distance; it seeped into the very fabric of their lives. The children were raised in an environment where loyalty to the crown was viewed with suspicion. As they grew, they were influenced by the revolutionary sentiments that surrounded them, complicating the queen's efforts to instill in them a sense of duty to their lineage. Marie Antoinette found herself grappling with the harsh reality that her children, her legacy, might be forever changed by the revolution—a reality that threatened to sever the bonds they had forged as a family.

In the depths of her despair, Marie Antoinette clung to the hope of reunion, the belief that she would one day reclaim her children and restore their lives to the way they once were. Yet, as the revolution raged on, that hope began to fade, replaced by the gnawing fear that she might never see them again. The walls of the Tuileries, which had once been a symbol of royal power and privilege, now felt like a prison, closing in around her.

The queen's final separation from her children came in August 1792, when they were moved to a different location amid growing unrest. Marie Antoinette was left with nothing but memories of their laughter, their innocent questions, and the warmth of their hugs. In those harrowing moments, she resolved to remain strong, believing that her love could transcend the barriers that had been erected between them. But the revolution had other plans, and the tragic twists of fate would soon seal their destinies in ways she could never have foreseen.

Amid the chaos, Marie Antoinette was left to grapple with her identity as a mother and a queen. The weight of her choices, the burdens of her past, and the impending doom of her future collided in a maelstrom of emotion. She was a woman torn between the love for her family and the relentless march of history that sought to redefine her legacy. In that darkened palace, stripped of her royal privileges and her children's embrace, she faced the ultimate test of a mother's love and a queen's resolve. The world outside raged on, but within her heart, the echoes of her family remained—a poignant reminder of what was lost and what she fought to preserve amidst the trials of her tragic existence.

The trial of Marie Antoinette stands as one of the most dramatic episodes in the tumultuous saga of the French Revolution, encapsulating the fall of an entire monarchy and the transition of a nation into uncharted territory. By the time her trial commenced, the political landscape of France had transformed irrevocably. The public, once enamored by the glamour of the court, had turned into a fervent mob demanding justice, often blinded by rage and revolutionary fervor. For Marie Antoinette, the once-revered queen, the tribunal represented not merely a legal proceeding but a stage for her public humiliation and a crucible for the turbulent emotions of a nation grappling with its identity.

As her trial began in October 1793, the atmosphere was rife with tension and hostility. The Revolutionary Tribunal, a new entity designed to expedite the prosecution of enemies of the state, was a product of the radical Jacobin influence. The court was presided over by a group of men who were not only politically motivated but also deeply influenced by the revolutionary zeal that had swept through France. They were determined to root out the vestiges of the old regime, and Marie Antoinette, as the embodiment of royal excess and privilege, was an irresistible target.

The queen entered the courtroom with a dignity that belied her dire circumstances. Though she had been stripped of her regal attire, her poise was unmistakable, a remnant of her former grandeur. However, the atmosphere was hostile. The court was packed with spectators, many of whom had come not to witness a fair trial but to partake in a spectacle, eager to see the fall of a once-mighty queen. The charges against her were sweeping and sensational, ranging from treason to conspiracy against the republic. Her accusers painted her as a foreign agent, a traitor who had conspired with Austria, her homeland, to undermine the revolution and restore the monarchy.

The prosecutor, Antoine Quentin Fouquier-Tinville, delivered his opening statements with fervor, presenting a narrative that sought to vilify Marie Antoinette as the very source of France's woes. He asserted that her extravagant lifestyle and alleged indifference to the suffering of the masses were emblematic of a queen who had lost touch with her people. Each accusation was met with gasps and murmurs from the audience, as the revolutionary fervor fueled their desire for retribution.

Marie Antoinette's defense was fraught with difficulties. The legal system was not designed for fairness; it served as a means to execute the will of the revolutionaries. The queen's attorney, an advocate named Antoine de Cazalès, attempted to counter the charges by emphasizing her role as a devoted mother and loyal wife, arguing that her actions had always been motivated by a desire to protect her family and her country. However, the court's predilection for condemnation overshadowed any pleas for mercy or understanding. The revolutionary tribunal had already rendered its verdict long before the trial even began; Marie Antoinette was guilty in the court of public opinion.

During the proceedings, Marie Antoinette remained remarkably composed, responding to questions with an air of defiance. She passionately denied the most shocking accusations, especially those involving her supposed involvement in a plot to aid Austria. "I have been falsely accused," she declared, her voice steady. "I am not a traitor." Yet, her words fell on deaf ears. The atmosphere was charged with animosity, and the revolutionary leaders, eager to solidify their power, were determined to make an example of her.

A particularly damning moment came when the court presented the testimony of various witnesses, many of whom were former courtiers or servants who had turned against her. Their accounts were laced with embellishments and animosity, painting her as a woman who reveled in the excesses of her position while the common people suffered. The contrast between her lavish lifestyle and the dire straits of the French populace was a narrative that resonated powerfully in a society that had experienced years of hardship. The queen's attempts to refute these claims were met with scorn, and her royal status seemed to work against her.

Amidst the barrage of accusations, one of the most shocking charges emerged: the claim that Marie Antoinette had sexually abused her own son, the young Louis Charles. This heinous allegation was designed to strip her of any remaining dignity and maternal image. The queen vehemently denied the accusation, declaring it to be a monstrous lie. However, the damage was done; the seeds of scandal had been planted, and they fed the revolutionary zeal that sought to destroy her.

As the trial progressed, it became clear that the revolutionaries were not merely seeking justice; they were conducting a political theater aimed at consolidating their power and stifling any opposition. Marie Antoinette's presence in the courtroom served as a reminder of the old order, and her execution would symbolize the definitive break from the past. The tribunal, rather than being a bastion of justice, had devolved into a vehicle for vengeance, and the queen stood at its center, a tragic figure ensnared by the very forces that had once celebrated her.

On October 14, 1793, after a trial that lasted merely a few days, the tribunal reached its verdict. Marie Antoinette was found guilty of treason, and the sentence was swift and merciless: death by guillotine. The news sent shockwaves through the nation, a culmination of hatred that had been festering for years. For many, her execution was seen as a necessary act of justice; for others, it marked the end of an era, a moment of profound loss that would echo throughout history.

In the months that followed, Marie Antoinette's trial and subsequent execution became a potent symbol of the revolution's darker turn. The queen's life, once filled with luxury and privilege, had descended into a tragic narrative of betrayal, scandal, and ultimately, the loss of her life. Her trial, a spectacle of public condemnation, would serve as a grim reminder of the price of power and the volatility of public opinion in a time of upheaval, encapsulating the complex legacy of a woman who would forever be remembered as both a queen and a victim of her times.

Chapter 10: The Final Days: Execution and Legacy

The air was thick with tension and uncertainty as Marie Antoinette faced the grim reality of her impending execution. The date was set for October 16, 1793, but the days leading up to it were a whirlwind of anxiety and despair. In the dimly lit confines of her prison cell at the Conciergerie, she could hear the distant echoes of revolution, the fervent cries of the people who had once celebrated her as a queen. Now, she was nothing more than a symbol of the monarchy's excesses, a scapegoat for the turmoil that had engulfed France.

On the morning of her execution, she was awoken early, the chill of autumn seeping through the stone walls. Clad in a simple white dress, stripped of the opulence that had once defined her, Marie Antoinette prepared to meet her fate. The transformation from queen to prisoner was stark; her once luxurious silks and grand gowns were replaced by the somber attire befitting a condemned woman. Her hair, once a tower of extravagant curls, was hastily cut short, a final act of defiance against the norms that had dictated her identity.

As she was led from her cell, the guards were brusque, their demeanor reflecting the tumultuous sentiment of the times. Yet, in that dark hour, Marie Antoinette maintained a semblance of dignity. She walked with her head held high, her spirit unbroken despite the palpable fear gripping her heart. The corridors of the Conciergerie were a far cry from the grand halls of Versailles, and yet, she moved through them as if they were a royal procession.

The streets of Paris outside were a cacophony of noise, a mix of shouts, jeers, and fervent revolutionary fervor. The populace had gathered, a sea of faces twisted by anger and anticipation, eager to witness the downfall of the queen they believed had drained their nation of its vitality. In their eyes, she was not the young girl who had once been sent from Austria to marry a future king, but a tyrant, a woman who had lived in luxurious excess while they suffered. The clattering of the carts and the murmurs of the crowd grew louder as Marie Antoinette approached the place of execution, the Place de la Révolution.

In the cart that transported her, she was flanked by guards and watched closely, but her mind was a torrent of memories. She thought of her children, of the days spent in the gardens of Versailles, of laughter and music, of the life that had been so violently taken from her. She recalled the fleeting moments of joy, now shadowed by the specter of her impending death. Each bump of the cart jolted her back to the present, where the reality of her situation was inescapable.

As the cart made its way through the streets, the tension in the air crackled with anticipation. The crowd surged like a tide, some shouting curses, while others observed in morbid fascination. Children were hoisted onto shoulders for a better view, their innocent faces reflecting the chaos of their parents' anger. Marie Antoinette, though terrified, felt a strange sense of calm. She had once been the embodiment of luxury and power, and now she was the embodiment of the fragility of life and the unpredictability of fate.

The cart finally halted, and she was escorted down to the scaffold. The sight of the guillotine, stark and imposing against the sky, was a grim reminder of the reality she faced. It was a symbol of the revolution's brutality, a tool of justice that had come to signify the end of an era. As she ascended the steps, the crowd's roar reached a fever pitch, a blend of excitement and anger that reverberated through the air.

At the foot of the guillotine, Marie Antoinette paused, taking a moment to gaze out upon the sea of faces, some filled with hatred, others with a grim curiosity. She sought a sliver of compassion, a flicker of understanding, but found none. There was no safety net, no escape from the judgment that loomed over her. In that moment, she felt the weight of her past decisions, the alliances made, the court intrigues, the luxury she had indulged in when her people struggled. The enormity of it all bore down on her, but she refused to succumb to despair.

As she took her place on the scaffold, she struggled to remain composed, her heart racing as she faced the executioner. In the final moments, she summoned the strength of the queen she had been, the mother she still was. With courage forged in the fires of adversity, she prepared to meet her end with grace. She uttered a prayer, a final plea for forgiveness, for peace, for her children.

The executioner approached, and with a swift motion, the blade fell. In an instant, Marie Antoinette's life was snuffed out, her body rendered lifeless, but her spirit, her story—one of luxury, scandal, and tragedy—would endure. The crowd erupted, some cheering for the end of a monarchy, while others were left with a profound silence, an understanding that they had witnessed not just the death of a queen, but the death of an era.

As the dust settled and the echoes of the crowd faded away, Marie Antoinette's legacy began to take shape. In death, she became a symbol of the complexities of power, the fragility of life, and the consequences of excess. The journey to the guillotine was not merely a passage to her death; it became an indelible moment in history, a poignant reminder of the woman who had once danced in the grand halls of Versailles, now silenced by the very revolution she had failed to understand.

As the sun rose on the fateful day of October 16, 1793, a heavy silence enveloped Paris. The air was charged with an unspoken tension, the kind that grips a city on the brink of monumental change. In the depths of the Conciergerie, Marie Antoinette prepared for what would be her final moments. The former queen, once adorned in silks and jewels, now faced the specter of death with a clarity that belied her earlier frivolities.

The queen's last hours were spent in the company of her loyal maid, who had stayed by her side through the tumultuous years. Marie Antoinette had always been a woman of remarkable resilience, but as she contemplated the reality of her execution, she drew upon all the strength she could muster. In her heart, she grappled with the weight of her past—the opulence of Versailles, the adulation of the court, and the infamous scandals that had marred her reputation. Yet, beneath the layers of her public persona, there lay a woman who was a devoted mother, a grieving widow, and ultimately, a tragic figure of history.

As she dressed for her execution, Marie Antoinette chose a simple white gown, a stark contrast to the extravagant attire that had once characterized her life. She would not go to her end draped in the finery of a queen; she would instead present herself as a woman stripped of her titles, facing her fate with dignity. In those final moments, she sought solace in the thought of her children, the only aspect of her life that had ever brought her true joy. Each thought of them was both a comfort and a source of profound sorrow; she had been separated from them for so long, and the thought of leaving them forever cut her to the core.

As she was led to the cart that would take her to the Place de la Révolution, the streets of Paris were lined with spectators, some curious, others eager to witness the downfall of a queen they believed had brought their nation to ruin. Marie Antoinette's heart raced, but she steeled herself, determined not to show fear. The cart was a simple vehicle, devoid of the splendor she once rode in. It was a poignant reminder of her fall from grace, a symbol of the revolution that had consumed her world.

Even in this moment of despair, Marie Antoinette's spirit shone through. As the cart moved slowly through the streets, she raised her head high, her demeanor regal yet somber. The jeers of the crowd reached her ears, but she remained steadfast, her mind resolute. She was determined to face her executioners with the dignity befitting a queen, even if she was no longer regarded as one by the people.

Upon reaching the scaffold, the atmosphere shifted; the crowd grew restless, charged with a mixture of anger, excitement, and anticipation. As she ascended the steps to the guillotine, the enormity of the moment bore down on her. The blade gleamed ominously in the sunlight, a stark reminder of the fate that awaited her. In that instant, Marie Antoinette's thoughts turned inward, and she found herself reflecting on the choices that had led her here. The political machinations, the alliances, the betrayals—all of it had culminated in this singular, tragic moment.

As she stood before the executioner, the weight of her impending death pressed heavily on her shoulders. Yet, she found the strength to speak, her voice steady despite the chaos around her. Her last words, whispered but clear, were directed toward the executioner. "Pardon me, sir; I did not mean to step on your foot." Though simple, her words spoke volumes about her character. Even in her final moments, she exhibited grace and compassion, unwilling to allow her final act to be filled with bitterness or malice.

The crowd, taken aback by her composure, momentarily fell silent, as if they were witnessing not just the execution of a queen but the extinguishing of a life full of contradictions—a life marked by both indulgence and suffering. In that fleeting moment, Marie Antoinette transcended the role of a fallen monarch; she became a symbol of humanity, a woman facing her mortality with courage.

As the executioner prepared to fulfill his grim duty, Marie Antoinette's thoughts turned once more to her children, to the legacy she would leave behind. She hoped they would know her not as the queen who lost her head but as a mother who loved fiercely, who had fought for their future even in the darkest of times. Perhaps they would remember her laughter, the moments of joy they had shared, and the dreams she had harbored for them.

The crowd stirred, anticipation rippling through the masses. With a swift motion, the blade fell, severing the ties of her earthly existence. A life once filled with luxury and scandal met its tragic end, leaving behind a complex legacy that would haunt France for generations to come.

In the aftermath, the echoes of Marie Antoinette's last words would resonate beyond the Place de la Révolution. They would become entwined with the narrative of her life—a life that had been a tapestry of contradictions. The woman who had once been derided as "Madame Deficit" would be remembered not only for her extravagance but also for her humanity, her final moments encapsulating the essence of a woman who had navigated the treacherous waters of power and loss.

As history would come to judge her, Marie Antoinette would remain a figure of both scorn and sympathy, a queen whose last words captured the essence of her tragic life—a life defined by love, loss, and ultimately, the unwavering strength of the human spirit.

The legacy of Marie Antoinette is as complex and multifaceted as the life she led, intertwining the opulence of her royal upbringing with the stark realities of the tumultuous period that ultimately led to her downfall. Her story is not merely one of a queen who lost her throne; it is emblematic of the broader societal shifts that swept through France and Europe during the late 18th century. As the daughter of Empress Maria Theresa of Austria, Marie Antoinette was born into a world of privilege and expectation, yet her life became a cautionary tale of excess, misjudgment, and tragedy.

One of the most enduring aspects of Marie Antoinette's legacy is her role as a symbol of the excesses of monarchy. In the years preceding the French Revolution, while the common citizens of France faced dire economic hardship, the queen's lavish lifestyle became the focus of public ire. The opulence of her court, epitomized by the splendid Petit Trianon and extravagant soirées filled with elaborate costumes and sumptuous banquets, stood in stark contrast to the struggles of the French populace. This disparity fueled resentment and became fertile ground for revolutionary sentiments. Her image as a frivolous and out-of-touch royal was solidified through pamphlets, caricatures, and gossip that painted her as the archetype of royal excess. The phrase "Let them eat cake," often misattributed to her, encapsulates the perception of her insensitivity to the plight of the poor, even though there is no evidence she ever uttered those words.

However, to view her solely through this lens of extravagance would be to ignore the complexities of her character and her efforts to navigate the turbulent waters of French politics. While she was often criticized for her spending habits and perceived aloofness, Marie Antoinette was also a woman of her time who faced immense pressure to uphold the dignity of the crown and secure her family's position. Her attempts to reform the royal household and engage with issues of governance were often thwarted by the entrenched interests of the French court and her own isolation as a foreign queen. In this light, her legacy becomes one of a tragic figure caught in the crosshairs of historical forces beyond her control.

The impact of Marie Antoinette's life and death extended far beyond the immediate aftermath of her execution. Following her death, she became a martyr for the royalist cause and a potent symbol of the Revolution's violent excesses. The guillotine, which claimed her life, became a stark emblem of not only the fall of the monarchy but also the radical transformation of French society. Her execution in October 1793 marked a watershed moment in the Revolution, representing the culmination of years of growing discontent and the radicalization of revolutionary ideals. In the eyes of royalists and sympathizers, Marie Antoinette was not merely a fallen queen; she was a victim of an unjust and brutal regime that turned on its own leaders in a frenzy of violence.

In the decades following her death, Marie Antoinette's legacy continued to evolve. Historians and biographers would grapple with her image, oscillating between the portrayal of a reckless spendthrift and a misunderstood woman trapped by her circumstances. Romanticized accounts of her life began to emerge, often focusing on her youth, beauty, and the tragic elements of her story. As the 19th century progressed, novels, plays, and operas began to depict her life with a sense of empathy, framing her as a tragic heroine rather than just a symbol of decadence. This shift in perception highlighted a growing interest in the personal narratives of historical figures, allowing for a more nuanced understanding of her character and motivations.

In the 20th century, the fascination with Marie Antoinette reached new heights, with various adaptations in literature and film. Directors and writers explored her life through different lenses, from the opulent and romantic to the critical and analytical. These portrayals often reflected contemporary societal issues, such as gender politics, class struggles, and the nature of power. The 2006 film "Marie Antoinette," directed by Sofia Coppola, reinvigorated interest in her life, presenting a visually stunning and emotionally resonant interpretation that sought to humanize the queen and explore her inner world. Such representations have helped to ensure that her story remains relevant, encouraging ongoing discourse about the implications of power, privilege, and public perception.

Moreover, Marie Antoinette's legacy has had a lasting impact on modern royalty and the perception of queens in contemporary society. As royal families navigate their roles in the public eye, the lessons drawn from her life resonate deeply. The scrutiny that modern royals face, often amplified by social media, echoes the intense public gaze that Marie Antoinette endured. Her struggles with identity, duty, and the relentless demands of her position continue to inform discussions about the responsibilities and challenges faced by those in power. In this sense, Marie Antoinette serves as a historical touchstone, a reminder of the delicate balance between privilege and public service, and the consequences that can arise when that balance is disrupted.

In the end, the legacy of Marie Antoinette is one of contrasts—a life defined by both opulence and isolation, influence and vulnerability. Her story is a poignant reminder of the complexities of human experience, illustrating how a single figure can embody the hopes, fears, and contradictions of an entire era. As we reflect on her life and legacy, we are reminded that history is not merely a collection of events but a tapestry woven from the lives of individuals who, despite their flaws and failings, continue to captivate our imagination and inspire reflection on the nature of power, identity, and humanity.

Chapter 11: Myth vs. Reality: The Legend of Marie Antoinette

Marie Antoinette has long been ensnared in a web of myths and misconceptions, many of which have overshadowed the complexities of her life and reign. From the infamous phrase "Let them eat cake" to the portrayal of her as a frivolous spendthrift, the image of the queen has been molded by sensationalism and propaganda. In examining the historical record, we find that many of these narratives, often repeated over generations, are far removed from the reality of her character and circumstances.

One of the most enduring myths about Marie Antoinette is her supposed indifference to the plight of the French people, encapsulated in the phrase, "Let them eat cake." This quote, attributed to her in the context of the French populace suffering from famine, paints her as callous and disconnected from reality. However, there is no credible evidence that she ever uttered these words. The phrase was actually coined by Jean-Jacques Rousseau in his autobiographical work, "Confessions," written in the mid-18th century, where he suggested that a princess had said it in response to the poor. Rousseau's comments were likely intended as a critique of the nobility's lack of awareness about the suffering of the lower classes, not as a direct indictment of Marie Antoinette herself. In truth, she was acutely aware of the economic hardships facing France and, in her later years, attempted to address these issues through various reforms and charitable efforts.

Moreover, while Marie Antoinette has been vilified as a spendthrift who squandered the nation's wealth on her lavish lifestyle, the reality is far more nuanced. As queen, she did indulge in opulence; the exquisite gowns, luxurious jewelry, and grand parties at Versailles have become part of her legend. Yet, much of her spending was also a reflection of the expectations of her role and the culture of the French court, where excess was the norm. Her expenditures were often scrutinized and exaggerated by political enemies seeking to undermine her influence. It is important to recognize that Marie Antoinette was not the sole architect of France's financial woes; rather, she was a scapegoat for deeper systemic issues within the monarchy that had been festering long before her arrival in France.

Another pervasive myth revolves around Marie Antoinette's relationship with her husband, King Louis XVI. Often depicted as a cold and distant union, the reality was more complex. Their marriage, arranged for political reasons, struggled initially, but over time, a genuine affection developed between them. Both were young and inexperienced when they married, and they faced immense pressure from their roles as monarchs. Their shared experiences of isolation in the unforgiving environment of the French court fostered a bond that, while challenged by political strife and personal tragedy, remained significant throughout their lives. Their efforts to produce an heir, although initially fraught with difficulty, ultimately resulted in the birth of four children, further solidifying their partnership.

The image of Marie Antoinette as an insatiable fashionista, obsessed solely with her appearance and status, simplifies the multifaceted nature of her identity. While it is true that she was a trendsetter, influencing fashion with her extravagant gowns and hairstyles, her interest extended beyond mere vanity. Fashion was an essential part of her role as queen; it was a means of expressing her status and fostering political alliances. In an environment where appearance held great significance, her carefully curated image served as both a shield and a tool. It is crucial to understand that her fashion choices were, in many ways, a reflection of the pressures and expectations imposed upon her by the court and society at large.

Equally misleading is the portrayal of Marie Antoinette as a foreign interloper, an Austrian outsider who never integrated into French society. This narrative, heavily fueled by nationalism and anti-Austrian sentiment, overlooks her attempts to assimilate and her genuine affection for France. Marie Antoinette embraced French customs and sought to learn the language, and she endeavored to cultivate relationships with her subjects through her patronage of the arts and charitable works. Her love for France was evident in her efforts to promote French culture, as seen in her support for the development of the arts and her involvement in various charitable initiatives aimed at improving the lives of the less fortunate.

Additionally, the notion that Marie Antoinette was solely responsible for the downfall of the monarchy is a gross oversimplification. While her actions and decisions have been scrutinized in the context of the Revolution, the roots of the conflict were deeply embedded in the socio-economic conditions of France. The Enlightenment, rising discontent among the bourgeoisie, and the financial mismanagement of the monarchy contributed to a climate ripe for revolution. Marie Antoinette, as a public figure, became emblematic of the excesses of the Old Regime, but she was not the architect of its demise. Instead, she was a victim of circumstances beyond her control, caught in a historical maelstrom that would ultimately lead to the collapse of the monarchy.

Lastly, the imagery of Marie Antoinette as a tragic figure is often romanticized, yet it is essential to recognize the agency she wielded throughout her life. While she faced insurmountable challenges and tragedies, including the loss of loved ones and her eventual execution, she also exhibited resilience and strength in the face of adversity. Her ability to navigate the treacherous waters of court politics, her devotion to her children, and her determination to maintain her dignity during her final days reveal a woman who, despite her flaws and vulnerabilities, possessed a remarkable inner strength.

In debunking the myths surrounding Marie Antoinette, we begin to uncover the layers of her character and the complexities of her life. She was a queen who navigated a tumultuous era, shaped by the expectations of her role, the realities of her circumstances, and the tumult of a nation on the brink of revolution. By understanding the truth behind the myths, we can appreciate not only the historical significance of her life but also the enduring legacy of a woman who has captivated imaginations for centuries.

Marie Antoinette's life has been a fertile ground for artistic interpretation and media portrayals, shaping and reshaping public perception of the queen over centuries. From the opulent canvases of the 18th century to modern films and television series, the image of Marie Antoinette has been both romanticized and vilified, reflecting the evolving attitudes toward monarchy, femininity, and power.

In the late 18th century, as revolution brewed in France, artists began to depict Marie Antoinette in ways that highlighted her status, beauty, and, often, extravagance. This was a time when portraiture served not only as an artistic endeavor but also as a means of political commentary. Artists like Élisabeth Louise Vigée Le Brun, Marie Antoinette's official portraitist, played a crucial role in crafting a public image that blended idealized beauty with royal dignity. Vigée Le Brun's portraits of the queen, adorned in luxurious gowns and often depicted in pastoral settings, sought to evoke an image of a benevolent and fashionable monarch, contrasting sharply with the growing discontent among the populace. These images were carefully curated to emphasize her connection to the people and her role as a devoted mother, often showcasing her with her children in intimate, tender moments—an attempt to soften her image amidst the rising tide of criticism.

Yet, the disconnect between the queen's lavish lifestyle and the hardships faced by the French populace was glaring. As the Revolution progressed, the art that depicted Marie Antoinette began to shift. The queen became a symbol of excess and decadence, and artists responded to the changing political landscape by portraying her in ways that expressed the anger and resentment of the common people. Satirical prints became rampant, often exaggerating her luxurious lifestyle and depicting her as a villainous figure detached from reality. In these works, she was not merely a queen but a representation of the old regime—opulent, out of touch, and ultimately deserving of the fate that awaited her. The biting caricatures of the time, such as those by Jacques-Louis David, served to amplify the revolutionary fervor, using art as a weapon against monarchy.

As the 19th century unfolded, Marie Antoinette's image continued to evolve. Romanticism brought a wave of interest in her tragic narrative, leading to a more sympathetic portrayal. Artists and writers began to emphasize her youth, beauty, and the pathos of her fate. Alexandre Dumas' historical fiction, alongside other literary works, painted the queen as a tragic heroine, a victim of circumstance rather than a tyrant. This shift was a reflection of a broader cultural fascination with individual suffering and the complexities of human emotion, highlighting the inherent tragedy of her life and death.

As the 20th century progressed, the depiction of Marie Antoinette in films and literature further diversified, often oscillating between glamorous fantasy and harsh reality. The film adaptations of her life have ranged from the lavish to the absurd, illustrating how her story can be interpreted through various lenses. Sofia Coppola's 2006 film, "Marie Antoinette," is perhaps the most notable example of this trend. It presents the queen as a misunderstood figure trapped in a gilded cage, a portrayal that resonates with contemporary audiences who see her not just as a queen but as a young woman grappling with isolation and the suffocating expectations of her role. The film's lush visuals and modern soundtrack created a fairy-tale atmosphere that contrasted sharply with the grim historical outcome, prompting discussions about the nature of identity, privilege, and rebellion against societal norms.

Television series and documentaries have also explored Marie Antoinette's life, further contributing to her complex legacy. These portrayals often seek to demystify her life, focusing not only on her opulence but also on her human struggles and resilience. The BBC series "Versailles" and the historical drama "Marie Antoinette," produced by various networks, delve into the intricacies of her relationships and the political machinations of the time, providing viewers with a more nuanced understanding of her character. The queen's story is often framed within the broader context of the French Revolution, allowing audiences to grasp the complexities of loyalty, betrayal, and the societal upheaval that marked her reign.

In parallel, popular culture has also embraced the notion of Marie Antoinette as a symbol of excess and rebellion, often using her as a reference point to critique contemporary issues such as consumerism and social inequality. Fashion designers, artists, and musicians have drawn inspiration from her life, using her iconic style as a canvas to express modern themes of femininity and power dynamics. The enduring fascination with her extravagant wardrobe—particularly her penchant for elaborate gowns and extravagant hairstyles—has made her a muse for fashion houses and artists alike, who reinterpret her image to comment on current societal issues.

However, while many portrayals have sought to humanize Marie Antoinette or criticize the monarchy, they often risk oversimplifying her life into mere caricature. The tendency to romanticize or vilify her obscures the complexities of her character and the socio-political realities of her time. As 21st-century audiences engage with her story, it becomes increasingly important to approach these portrayals with a critical eye, recognizing the layers of myth and reality that have shaped her legacy.

Ultimately, the various representations of Marie Antoinette in art and media reveal not just the queen's personal narrative but also the shifting perceptions of monarchy and femininity across time. She remains a symbol of both luxury and tragedy, a figure whose life encapsulates the tensions between personal desires and public expectations. As we dissect these portrayals, we must acknowledge the ways in which they reflect our own cultural beliefs and values, ensuring that the legacy of Marie Antoinette continues to provoke thought and discussion long after her tragic end.

Marie Antoinette's life and legacy have long captivated the imagination of not just historians but also artists, filmmakers, and writers. As one of history's most enigmatic figures, she has been transformed from a misunderstood queen into a cultural icon, often serving as a canvas upon which society projects its notions of femininity, power, luxury, and tragedy. This subchapter explores how Marie Antoinette has been represented in popular culture, revealing the complexities and contradictions of her character as well as the enduring fascination she evokes.

The portrayal of Marie Antoinette in literature and art began almost immediately after her death in 1793, with writers and artists eager to capitalize on the sensationalism surrounding her story. One of the earliest accounts came from the pen of Alexandre Dumas, who, in the 19th century, rendered her life into a romanticized narrative, focusing on her beauty and the excesses of her court. Dumas's depiction established a template for future portrayals, one that emphasized the glamorous yet tragic aspects of her existence. This narrative of opulence coupled with downfall would resonate through the ages, as it reflected both the desires and fears of an evolving society.

Throughout the 20th century, Marie Antoinette's image was further immortalized through various artistic interpretations. In the realm of visual art, she has been the subject of countless paintings, sculptures, and installations. Notably, the works of the French painter Élisabeth Louise Vigée Le Brun, who painted portraits of the queen that emphasized her elegance and maternal qualities, remain some of the most recognizable images associated with her. Vigée Le Brun's portraits not only captured Marie Antoinette's physical beauty but also sought to present her in a more favorable light, countering the negative public perception that arose during her reign.

As the 20th century progressed, the fascination with Marie Antoinette took on new dimensions in cinema and literature. The 1938 film "Marie Antoinette," directed by W.S. Van Dyke, offered a lush and romanticized depiction of the queen, showcasing her lavish lifestyle and tragic end. Starring Norma Shearer, the film painted a portrait of a woman trapped by the expectations of her time, a theme that would resonate with audiences for decades. The portrayal emphasized the idea of Marie Antoinette as a victim of circumstance, a narrative that softened the edges of her extravagant reputation.

In stark contrast, Sofia Coppola's 2006 film "Marie Antoinette" presented a modern and stylized interpretation of the queen's life. With a contemporary soundtrack and vibrant visuals, Coppola's film infused the historical figure with a sense of youth and rebellion. The film depicted Marie Antoinette as a misunderstood adolescent thrust into a world of political intrigue and unattainable expectations. The use of modern music alongside the sumptuous imagery of Versailles created a striking juxtaposition, making her struggles feel relatable to a contemporary audience. Coppola's depiction of Marie Antoinette as a figure of both privilege and isolation resonated with viewers, raising questions about the nature of freedom and identity.

In literature, the fascination with Marie Antoinette has inspired numerous novels, ranging from historical fiction to speculative retellings. Authors such as Antonia Fraser and Carolly Erickson have delved into the queen's life, aiming to provide a more nuanced understanding of her character. Fraser's biography, "Marie Antoinette: The Journey," is particularly notable for its attempt to humanize the queen, exploring her personal struggles, relationships, and the political pressures she faced. By providing a well-researched account, Fraser invites readers to reconsider the often one-dimensional portrayals of Marie Antoinette that dominate popular culture.

Moreover, the queen has become an emblematic figure in the realm of fashion. Her influence continues to be felt in the world of haute couture, where designers often draw inspiration from her extravagant style. The iconic image of Marie Antoinette, with her elaborate gowns and towering hairstyles, has become synonymous with notions of luxury and femininity. Fashion exhibitions, such as those held at the Metropolitan Museum of Art, have celebrated her impact on style, showcasing the intricate details of her wardrobe and emphasizing her role as a fashion icon of her era.

In the realm of social media, Marie Antoinette has found new life as a subject of memes, TikTok videos, and Instagram posts. The juxtaposition of her opulent lifestyle with contemporary commentary on wealth and privilege has sparked discussions about the relevance of her story in today's world. The phrase "Let them eat cake," often attributed to her, has been reinterpreted in various contexts, reflecting modern societal concerns about class disparity and the responsibilities of those in power. This digital renaissance has allowed a younger generation to engage with her legacy in a way that is both playful and critical, underscoring the multifaceted nature of her character.

Marie Antoinette's representation in popular culture serves as a powerful reminder of how history is often reshaped to fit contemporary narratives. While the queen's life was marked by luxury and excess, it was also characterized by deep personal struggles and societal pressures. Through art, literature, and film, her story has transcended time, allowing each generation to find its own meaning in her life and legacy. As a subject of fascination, Marie Antoinette continues to challenge perceptions of femininity, power, and tragedy, leaving an indelible mark on the cultural landscape. Ultimately, her enduring presence in popular culture invites us to reflect on the complexities of identity and the often-unforgiving nature of history itself.

Chapter 12: Reflections on a Life of Contrasts

Marie Antoinette's life epitomizes the juxtaposition of luxury and loss, a saga woven through the fabric of her existence that has left an indelible mark on history. Born into the opulence of the Habsburg dynasty, she was a princess surrounded by extravagance, yet her life was marred by profound personal and political tragedies. The stark contrasts that defined her story invite reflection on the complexities of her legacy, challenging the narratives shaped by both her contemporaries and historians alike.

In her early years, Marie Antoinette enjoyed a childhood steeped in privilege, living in the resplendent palaces of Vienna, where the grandeur of the Habsburg court enveloped her. The tapestries that adorned the walls, the sumptuous feasts, and the elaborate balls were all part of her formative experiences, shaping her understanding of royalty and expectation. Yet, this gilded upbringing came with its own burdens. As the youngest daughter of Empress Maria Theresa, she was groomed for political alliances rather than personal happiness. Her fate was sealed in the marriage negotiations that would take her from Austria to France, thrusting her into an unfamiliar world where she would be both a pawn and a player in the intricate game of monarchy.

Upon her arrival in France, Marie Antoinette was introduced to the splendor of Versailles, a palace that symbolized the zenith of French luxury. Here, she embraced her role as queen with fervor, quickly becoming known for her extravagant lifestyle that often drew the ire of the public. The lavish parties at the Petit Trianon, her personal retreat, showcased her penchant for excess, with opulent gowns, extravagant jewelry, and extravagant celebrations that seemed to defy the economic realities faced by many of her subjects. Critics labeled her as "Madame Deficit," a moniker that encapsulated the growing resentment towards her seemingly insatiable appetite for luxury. Yet, this external criticism often overshadowed the internal struggles she faced as a young woman navigating the treacherous waters of court politics and public scrutiny.

Marie Antoinette's indulgences were not merely acts of vanity; they were also expressions of identity and agency in a world where her autonomy was limited. In the throes of personal loss—particularly the early deaths of her children—she sought solace in the material comforts that surrounded her. The loss of her beloved children, particularly the tragic death of her youngest son, Louis Joseph, plunged her into deep despair. In these moments of grief, the opulence that had once enveloped her felt like a gilded cage, offering no solace from the emotional turmoil that accompanied her role as a mother and queen. This poignant contradiction—living in the lap of luxury while grappling with profound sorrow—paints a portrait of a woman whose life was anything but straightforward.

As the political climate in France grew increasingly volatile, Marie Antoinette's life became a study in the complexities of power and vulnerability. The very luxury that had defined her existence became a double-edged sword. The extravagant lifestyle of the royal court served as a focal point for public discontent, amplifying the cries for reform and revolution. The growing financial crisis in France, exacerbated by years of war and mismanagement, turned the queen into a symbol of excess at a time when the populace was struggling for basic sustenance. The glimmering jewels that adorned her neck became shackles of disdain, and the grandeur of Versailles morphed into a fortress of isolation.

In the face of this turmoil, Marie Antoinette's attempts at reform often fell flat, further complicating her legacy. Although she initiated efforts to alleviate the suffering of the poor and sought to modernize the monarchy, these efforts were often overshadowed by her extravagant reputation. Her attempts to connect with the French people were met with skepticism, as the gulf between the monarchy and the masses widened. This disconnect ultimately contributed to her downfall, revealing the harsh reality that even the most lavish life could not shield her from the consequences of political change.

As the Revolution erupted, Marie Antoinette's world unraveled. The opulence of her past became a distant memory as she faced the grim reality of imprisonment and impending doom. The palace that once echoed with laughter and celebration became a prison of despair, where she was stripped of her identity and dignity. The queen who had once commanded the admiration of her subjects now stood vilified, her luxurious lifestyle turned into a narrative of excess and irresponsibility. The contrast between her former life and her harrowing present underscored the fragility of power and the fleeting nature of fortune.

In the final days of her life, as she approached the guillotine, the complexity of her legacy became painfully evident. Marie Antoinette's execution marked the culmination of a life defined by both luxury and profound loss. Stripped of her royal trappings, she faced her fate with a resilience that belied her earlier excesses. Her last words, reportedly an apology to her executioner for stepping on his foot, encapsulated the tragic irony of her existence—a queen reduced to a moment of humanity in the face of death.

Today, Marie Antoinette's legacy continues to evoke intrigue and debate.

Historians and scholars grapple with the contradictions of her life, assessing her role as both a symbol of royal excess and a victim of circumstance. The luxury that once characterized her existence is often viewed through the lens of her tragic end, prompting reflections on the broader implications of power, privilege, and the human experience. In an age where the excesses of the elite remain a point of contention, her story resonates as a cautionary tale—a reminder that the trappings of wealth do not shield one from the tides of fate.

Marie Antoinette's life, marked by the stark contrasts of luxury and loss, invites us to ponder the complexities of human existence. Her legacy serves as both a reflection of the opulent world she inhabited and a testament to the trials she endured. In understanding her story, we uncover not just the life of a queen, but the universal themes of ambition, vulnerability, and the relentless pursuit of belonging in a world often divided by class and circumstance. Ultimately, her life is a poignant reminder that beneath the layers of extravagance lies the intricate tapestry of human emotion, frailty, and the enduring quest for meaning amidst the chaos of existence.

Marie Antoinette remains one of history's most iconic figures, her life a tapestry woven with threads of opulence, scandal, and tragedy. Yet, beyond the layers of myth and the sensationalism that often obscures her true character, her influence on modern royalty is palpable, echoing through the halls of palaces and the lives of contemporary leaders. The lessons drawn from her reign and her ultimate downfall continue to resonate, providing both cautionary tales and insights into the evolving role of monarchs in the modern world.

At the heart of Marie Antoinette's legacy is the notion of public perception and its profound impact on the institution of monarchy. Her life illustrates the delicate balance that royal figures must maintain between their personal lives and public expectations. In an age where the press and social media can shape narratives in the blink of an eye, today's royals are acutely aware of the power of public opinion. Much like Marie, who faced intense scrutiny over her lavish lifestyle, modern monarchs understand that their actions are constantly under the microscope. The shift towards transparency, where royals engage with their subjects and share aspects of their personal lives, can be seen as a direct response to the lessons drawn from Marie Antoinette's reign.

Marie's image as the extravagant queen, often depicted as out of touch with the struggles of her people, serves as an enduring reminder of the dangers of disconnect. The French Revolution was fueled in part by the populace's perception of a monarchy that was blind to the suffering of the common man. In contrast, contemporary royal families, such as the

British and the Swedish, have sought to present themselves as relatable figures. They engage in charitable work, advocate for social causes, and often share candid glimpses of their lives through social media. This effort to foster a more approachable image is a protective mechanism, aimed at ensuring the monarchy remains relevant and respected.

Furthermore, the significance of familial ties within royal households has been reexamined in light of Marie Antoinette's experiences. Her profound sense of loss, particularly in the separation from her children during her imprisonment, underscores the importance of family as a support system. Today's royals often prioritize their roles as parents, showcasing the significance of family values amidst their public duties. The emotional toll of her imprisonment and the tragic fate of her family reflect the vulnerability inherent within the royal experience. As such, modern monarchs often strive to present themselves as devoted parents, emphasizing that their familial relationships are as important as their public personas.

Moreover, Marie Antoinette's journey reflects the power dynamics within royal marriages. Initially seen as a political alliance meant to solidify relations between France and Austria, her marriage to Louis XVI was fraught with challenges, highlighting the complexities of love, duty, and expectation. Today, while royal marriages still serve political purposes, there is a palpable shift towards personal choice and compatibility. The narratives surrounding the marriages of figures like Prince Harry and Meghan Markle or Crown Princess Victoria of Sweden illustrate a departure from traditional expectations. These unions are grounded in love and mutual respect, signifying a modern understanding of partnership that honors both personal happiness and royal duty.

In addition to personal relationships, Marie Antoinette's legacy extends to the fashion and cultural influence of royalty. Her status as a fashion icon, often criticized during her lifetime, underscores the evolving relationship between royalty and style. Today's royals are keenly aware of their sartorial choices and their implications. Fashion has become a powerful tool for self-expression and cultural representation, allowing modern royals to connect with their subjects on a more personal level. The carefully curated wardrobes of figures like Kate Middleton and Queen Letizia reflect not only personal taste but also a consciousness of their role as influencers in contemporary society. This shift from opulence to relatability in royal fashion mirrors the lessons from Marie Antoinette's life, serving as a reminder that style can be both a statement of individuality and a reflection of cultural values.

The scrutiny faced by Marie Antoinette during her reign also draws parallels with the modern challenges of navigating crisis and controversy.

The missteps of a royal can quickly escalate into public relations disasters, much like the Diamond Necklace Affair that tarnished her reputation. Today's royals face similar challenges, often needing to manage public relations with deftness and care. The importance of crisis management, transparency, and accountability has never been more crucial, as the consequences of missteps can resonate far beyond the palace walls.

Moreover, the narrative surrounding Marie Antoinette's downfall serves as a cautionary tale about the fragility of power. The revolution that led to her execution was not merely a rejection of monarchy but a profound societal shift that questioned traditional hierarchies. Modern royalty must navigate a world where the concepts of power and privilege are continually being redefined. The rise of democratic ideals and the questioning of authority compel contemporary monarchs to reflect on their roles and responsibilities, ensuring they contribute positively to society rather than remain relics of a bygone era.

In the realm of philanthropy, Marie Antoinette's efforts to support charitable causes, though often overlooked, laid groundwork that modern royals have built upon. The importance of engaging with social issues has become a hallmark of contemporary royalty, with many modern-day royals dedicating themselves to various charitable foundations and advocacy work. This commitment to social causes reflects an understanding that true leadership involves more than mere ceremonial duties; it requires a genuine investment in the well-being of the community.

In essence, Marie Antoinette's life and legacy continue to shape the contours of modern royalty. Her experiences serve as a lens through which contemporary royals examine their roles, responsibilities, and relationships with their subjects. The lessons of empathy, humility, and the necessity for connection with the populace are as relevant now as they were in the 18th century. As modern monarchs navigate the complexities of their positions, they carry with them the echoes of a queen whose life was marked by both extravagance and tragedy, reminding us that the path of royalty is as much about the heart as it is about the crown.

Marie Antoinette's life, steeped in luxury and tragedy, serves as a poignant reminder of the complexities of human existence and the often harsh realities that accompany privilege. Despite being one of history's most vilified figures, her experiences and the choices she made offer numerous lessons that transcend the confines of her era. To reflect on her life is to engage with the broader themes of power, identity, and resilience, which continue to resonate in contemporary society.

One of the most significant lessons to glean from Marie Antoinette's life is the precarious nature of public perception. As the Queen of France, she was subject to the whims of the populace, her every action scrutinized and often distorted. The notorious phrase "Let them eat cake," falsely attributed to her, encapsulates the tendency of society to simplify and vilify those in positions of power. This misunderstanding of her character illustrates how the narrative surrounding a public figure can be shaped by political motives and social unrest. In today's digital age, where social media can amplify misinformation at an unprecedented scale, the lesson remains clear: public perception can be a double-edged sword. It can elevate a figure to iconic status or lead to their downfall, often regardless of their actual deeds or intentions.

Marie Antoinette's experience also highlights the importance of adaptability in the face of change. Initially, she arrived in France as a naïve young woman, unaccustomed to the intricate and often ruthless world of court politics. However, as she navigated her new life, she learned to wield her influence, becoming a fashion icon and a symbol of the monarchy. Yet, her inability to adapt to the changing political landscape of France ultimately contributed to her tragic fate. The lesson here is that while the ability to adapt is essential for survival, it must be matched with an awareness of one's environment and the willingness to evolve. In both personal and professional realms, recognizing the need for change and responding accordingly is vital for long-term success.

Furthermore, Marie Antoinette's tumultuous relationship with her identity speaks to the struggle many face in reconciling personal desires with societal expectations. As a foreign queen, she grappled with the weight of representing not only herself but also her homeland. The pressure to embody the ideals of French royalty while maintaining her Austrian heritage led to a profound internal conflict. Her attempts to forge a unique identity within the rigid confines of the French court often resulted in public disdain. This reflects a universal truth: the journey towards self-acceptance can be fraught with challenges, especially when navigating societal norms. In a world that still grapples with issues of identity and belonging, her story encourages individuals to embrace their complexities and resist the urge to conform to external expectations at the expense of their true selves.

Another vital lesson from her life is the importance of compassion and empathy. Despite her lavish lifestyle, there were moments when Marie Antoinette demonstrated genuine concern for her subjects. During her reign, she initiated charitable efforts, particularly in times of famine. However, her efforts often went unnoticed amidst the growing discontent surrounding her extravagant lifestyle. This dichotomy serves as a reminder that intentions can be overshadowed by perception—an important consideration for anyone in a position of authority. Leaders today can learn from her experience that actions must align with public sentiment and that true compassion must be coupled with humility. Demonstrating empathy towards marginalized communities and being attuned to their needs is essential to building trust and fostering connection.

Moreover, Marie Antoinette's tumultuous marriage to Louis XVI sheds light on the complexities of partnership and the interplay of personal and political motives. Their union, initially forged for political stability, evolved into a relationship marked by distance and misunderstanding. While they were devoted to their children, their inability to present a united front during the tumultuous years leading up to the Revolution ultimately weakened their position. The lesson here revolves around the significance of communication and mutual support within relationships. In any partnership, especially those under public scrutiny, cultivating open dialogue and understanding is crucial for navigating challenges and sustaining a united front.

Tragedy, too, plays a central role in the narrative of Marie Antoinette's life, providing a stark reminder of the fragility of existence. Her gradual descent from opulence to imprisonment and eventual execution underscores the unpredictability of fate. Life can change in an instant, often beyond our control. This inevitability challenges individuals to embrace the present moment and to cultivate resilience in the face of adversity. Marie Antoinette's tragic end serves as a cautionary tale about the impermanence of power and the importance of cherishing relationships and experiences while they last.

Lastly, perhaps the overarching lesson from Marie Antoinette's life is the enduring impact of legacy. Despite her tragic fate, her story continues to captivate modern audiences, sparking interest and debate about her life choices and the broader societal issues of her time. Her legacy extends beyond the confines of historical narrative; it informs discussions about the role of women, the nature of power, and the consequences of societal upheaval. In this way, her life serves as a canvas upon which future generations can reflect on their own values and choices. The narratives we construct about ourselves and the legacies we leave behind are profoundly influential, shaping perceptions long after we are gone.

In conclusion, the life of Marie Antoinette offers a rich tapestry of lessons that extend far beyond her era. Her experiences invite reflection on the nature of power, identity, and compassion. As individuals navigate the complexities of their own lives, they would do well to consider the multifaceted legacy of this enigmatic queen—a legacy that reminds us of the importance of adaptability, empathy, and the pursuit of authenticity amidst the tumult of life's challenges. The lessons drawn from her tragic existence resonate across time, encouraging introspection and growth in a world that continues to grapple with the themes she embodied.

Printed in Dunstable, United Kingdom